KINGDOM COMMERCE

LEADERS IMPACTING CULTURE THROUGH FAITH AND ACTION

U. S. Christian Chamber of Commerce

Kingdom Commerce: Leaders Impacting Culture through Faith and Action
Copyright © 2024 Compilation of the U. S. Christian Chamber of Commerce

All rights reserved. No part of this publication may be reproduced, distributed or transmitted in any form or by any means, including photocopying, recording, or other electronic or mechanical methods, without the prior written permission of the publisher, except in the case of brief quotations embodied in critical reviews and certain other noncommercial uses permitted by copyright law. For permission requests, write to the publisher, addressed "Attention: Permissions Coordinator," at the address above.

Scripture quotations marked (AMP) are taken from The Amplified® Bible, Copyright © 2015 by The Lockman Foundation, La Habra, CA 90631. All rights reserved. For Permission to Quote information visit http://www.lockman.org/

Scripture quotations marked (ESV) are taken from the ESV® Bible (The Holy Bible, English Standard Version®). ESV® Text Edition: 2016. Copyright © 2001 by Crossway, a publishing ministry of Good News Publishers. The ESV® text has been reproduced in cooperation with and by permission of Good News Publishers. Unauthorized reproduction of this publication is prohibited. All rights reserved.

Scripture quotations marked (KJV) are taken from the King James Version, which is in the public domain.

Scripture quotations marked (NASB) are from the (NASB®) New American Standard Bible®, Copyright © 1960, 1971, 1977, 1995, 2020 by The Lockman Foundation. Used by permission. All rights reserved. www.lockman.org

Scripture quotations marked (NIV) are taken from the Holy Bible, NEW INTERNATIONAL VERSION® NIV® Copyright © 1973, 1978, 1984, 2011 by Biblica, Inc.® Used by permission. All rights reserved worldwide.

Scripture quotations marked (NKJV) are taken from the New King James Version®. Copyright © 1982 by Thomas Nelson. Used by permission. All rights reserved.

Scripture quotations marked (NLT) are taken from the *Holy Bible,* New Living Translation, copyright © ©1996, 2004, 2007, 2013, 2015 by Tyndale House Foundation. Used by permission of Tyndale House Publishers Inc., Carol Stream, Illinois 60188. All rights reserved.

HigherLife Publishing & Marketing
PO Box 623307
Oviedo, FL 32762
HigherLifePublishing.com

In this publication, the term "Kingdom" is consistently capitalized to denote its special significance in reference to the Kingdom of God. This stylistic choice is made out of reverence and to honor the profound respect the U.S. Christian Chamber of Commerce holds for the Kingdom as the realm of God's sovereign rule and the community of His people. While this capitalization may differ from standard publishing practices, it is a deliberate decision to reflect the depth of its meaning within our faith and the mission of our organization.

Kingdom Commerce: Leaders Impacting Culture through Faith and Action
U. S. Christian Chamber of Commerce with Various authors
ISBN: HB 9798989529490
ISBN: PB 9798989940165
LOC: 1-13510039551
Printed in the United States of America
10 9 8 7 6 5 4 3 2 1

CONTENTS

Introduction v

Chapter 1 The Kingdom Advantage: Christian Leadership in Business by Howard Partridge...................... 1

Chapter 2 Rediscovering Identity: Rooting Business in Christ by Dawn Sipley... 5

Chapter 3 Christ-Centered Foundations: Building Enterprises on Eternal Values by Ford Taylor.............. 9

Chapter 4 Led by the Spirit by David Roznowski........................15

Chapter 5 Unveiling the Intangibles: Infusing the Fruits of the Spirit into Business by Joy Capps 19

Chapter 6 Miraculous Moments in Business: Recognizing God's Hand at Work by Morris Hartley......................25

Chapter 7 Cultivating a Godly Workforce: Building Teams Aligned with Christ's Values by Virginia Grounds.....29

Chapter 8 Ethics, Excellence, and Betrayal by Jim Subers...........33

Chapter 9 From Local to Global: The Transformative Power of Kingdom Thinking and Enterprise by William A. Snell Jr..39

Chapter 10 Navigating Modern Markets with Ancient Wisdom: 1 Corinthians 3, a Biblical Blueprint for Kingdom Commerce by Krystal Parker 45

Chapter 11   Refiner's Fire: Sanctification by Obedience ... or Disobedience by Simon Bois 49

Chapter 12   Integrating Worship: The Role of Praise and Prayer in Business by Dr. Joshua Steinke 57

Chapter 13   That They May Be One: The Power of Kingdom Collaboration by Jim & Martha Brangenberg 61

Chapter 14   Divine Appointments: Seizing God's Ordained Opportunities by Dana A. Dunmyer 65

Chapter 15   Strengthening Spiritual Bonds: The Heart of Christian Collaboration by Nicole L. Davis, PhD 69

Chapter 16   Transformative Business Practices: Crafting a Kingdom Paradigm for Success by Robert Fukui 73

Chapter 17   Mission-Driven Ventures: Aligning Business Goals with Heavenly Purpose by Craig Hohnberger 83

Chapter 18   Personal Spiritual Growth: Refining the Soul through Business Challenges by Bob Willbanks 89

Chapter 19   Unified in Mission: Crafting a Collective Christian Business Vision by Steve Ahearn 95

Chapter 20   The Future Awaits: Embracing God's Vision for Kingdom Entrepreneurs by Joy Dawson 99

Chapter 21   The Power of Identity: Understanding Who We Are in Christ by Chet Gladkowski 103

Chapter 22   Building to Last: Foundations in Jesus for Enduring Success by Ford Taylor 109

Chapter 23 Building Bridges: Connecting Commerce with
            Your Business Story by David Welday 117

Chapter 24 Shining Lights: Role Models in Christian Business
            Leadership by Nate Chrisman 123

Chapter 25 Growth and Grace: Trusting God to Determine
            Your Steps by Eric Floyd 127

Chapter 26 Faithful Stewardship: Managing Resources God's
            Way by Shelsea Becker 131

Chapter 27 Resilience and Restoration: Overcoming Setbacks
            with Faith by Eileen Vazquez 137

Chapter 28 God's View of Economy vs. Worldview: Purposeful
            Profit and Divine Distribution by Kristi Nowrouzi .. 141

Chapter 29 Our Daily Work—a Holy Calling to
            Stewardship—Serving the Lord Full Time by Jan
            Sturesson 147

Chapter 30 Visionary Ventures: Anticipating the Future of
            Kingdom Commerce by Steve Ahearn 151

Call to Action 155

What's Next? 155

Appendix A Workplace Theology 157

Appendix B Contributing Authors in Alphabetical Order 165

About the U.S. Christian Chamber of Commerce 185

INTRODUCTION

Welcome to a journey of transformation, wisdom, and faith-driven success.

As president of the U.S. Christian Chamber of Commerce, I have had the unique privilege of witnessing firsthand the extraordinary ways in which Christian CEOs and business leaders outperform their peers, not just in profitability, but in creating a culture that reflects the heart of Christ. *Kingdom Commerce: Leaders Impacting Culture through Faith and Action* was born out of our ongoing mission to advance the Kingdom of God, strengthen Christian businesses, and transform cities across the nation.

Culture is often shaped by stories. These narratives are powerful and compelling, not just as testimonies of faith but as beacons of hope and models of success in the marketplace. Our collective aim is to redeem the world of work for Kingdom advancement to forge a common language and mission that reclaims our nation for Christ.

Anchored in the principles of 1 Corinthians 3, this book holds profound insights for business owners today. Each author shares their own remarkable journey of challenges, faith, and growth. As you read, keep a Bible and a notebook close at hand. Reflect on the wisdom, embrace the triumphs, and absorb the lessons contained within.

Before you start each chapter, take a moment to pray. Ask God to renew your spirit, to give you fresh insight, wisdom, and a renewed reliance on Him. This book should not just be read; it should be experienced and acted upon. Share it, apply its timeless wisdom to your business and life, and watch how God moves in incredible ways.

May your journey through these pages be as enriching and transformative as the stories themselves. Enjoy the adventure, and may it ignite in you a passion to lead, serve, and prosper in God's divine purpose.

In Christ's love and service,

Krystal Parker

President, U.S. Christian Chamber of Commerce

CHAPTER 1
THE KINGDOM ADVANTAGE: CHRISTIAN LEADERSHIP IN BUSINESS

Howard Partridge

As a believer, you know there is advantage in knowing Christ—God's Holy Spirit is inside you! Further, if you are a mature believer, you seek to build up His Kingdom. However, it sometimes seems that being in business conflicts with being a believer. You need to generate income, but you want to avoid the love of money. You want to lead people, but you want your actions to be seasoned with grace. You want to grow, but you don't want to pursue selfish goals.

I know how you feel. I started my first business almost forty years ago. Three years later, I came to know Christ and got heavily involved in ministry. I began to feel like I should go into "full-time ministry." I wanted everyone in the world to know the joy of the miraculous life one could have in Christ.

I felt that focusing my time, energy, and money on building a business was "worldly" and that I was wasting *ministry* time by building my business. I wanted to be as pure and as active as I could for God and His Kingdom. I was about to join my mentors on a trip to Hong Kong when everything fell apart. The leader of the ministry I loved was leading a counseling session with me and my wife. Although he was a very experienced leader, missionary, church builder, and even a somewhat famous figure in the Christian world, he made a rookie's mistake in that meeting.

My wife and I were at odds about some family issues, and I asked him to help us. He had always been a patient listener and asked great questions. He was brilliant at getting to the root, rather than dealing with just the fruit. But on this day, he didn't take the time to ask any questions that would have helped him understand where my wife was coming from. He made no effort to meet her where she was. Instead, after hearing us both out, he made a harsh statement that completely shut her down.

He was accustomed to dealing with me, which was completely different. My attitude toward coaching and counseling was to be wide open. If there was something I was missing, I wanted it yanked out by the root! But you have to understand that my wife is Italian. From New Jersey. Pause there for a second. Not exactly the submissive type. And yet, she is very wise. She has what you might call "street smarts."

When he told her that she had "problems," she asked him to leave. After closing the door behind him, she turned to me and told me I had a choice: "Him or me." Although the decision wasn't a difficult one, the journey forward was. I chose my wife and my son. At the time, I thought I was choosing my family over the ministry, but I wasn't.

Fortunately, there were other leaders in that ministry that loved us and ministered to us. One of those men mentored me in leadership, and in time, I realized that my business *was* my full-time ministry. Since then, many team members, clients, and vendors have been saved and helped. As I learned how to lead, my business grew, and others wanted to know how I was building it.

I began coaching and training business owners on my methods over twenty-five years ago. Along the way, I became the first founding member of the John Maxwell Team and spent a lot of time with John in his highest-level mentoring programs. John says, "Leadership is influence," and the way you gain influence in someone else's life is by "adding value to them."

Along the way, my training/coaching company became the exclusive small business coaching company for the Zig Ziglar Corporation. Zig said, "You can have everything in life you want, if you will just help enough other people get what they want." When he was still with us, I used to tease him a bit about that statement by telling him that he "stole" it from Jesus. Jesus said, "Give and it will be given back to you, pressed down, shaken together and running over." In response, Zig would roar with his signature laugh, and say, "Well, I know Him personally, so that'll be okay!"

Dave Ramsey has endorsed a couple of my books too, and I've spent time learning his philosophy. In fact, I've learned from more people than I can count. Through those experiences and leading a worldwide community of business owners, leaders, and coaches, I've learned that the Bible has already taught us what Christian leadership is all about—*love*.

Tom Ziglar wrote a book called *10 Leadership Virtues for Disruptive Times*. AI, VR, and other technologies make it difficult to navigate leadership today. These "helps" have made it so you don't even know for sure what is true and what is not! Interestingly, the ten virtues Tom outlines in his book are the ten virtues found in the "love" chapter of the Bible—1 Corinthians 13.

Leadership is loving others. Scripture tells us to love the Lord and love others. Romans 13 even describes what love is! When we walk by the Spirit, we will experience the fruit of the Spirit. The chief one being LOVE! Love never fails. God Himself is Love. His Spirit loves *through* us. When you allow Christ to live—and love—through you, you will have a leadership advantage!

Several years ago, at a leadership conference in Puerto Rico, I got to spend some time with the spiritual giant, Dr. Henry Blackaby. His book, *Experiencing God,* had sold something like *nine million* copies at that time. I got to spend time with the man who had been invited to the White House to counsel four sitting presidents for three days in a row! At that time, he and his son Richard were mentoring CEOs that ran companies earning a minimum of $100 million per year!

In their book, *Spiritual Leadership*, Henry and Richard Blackaby make this statement: "Leaders who know God and know how to lead in a Christian manner will be *phenomenally* more effective in their world than the most skilled and qualified leaders who lead without God."[1]

Henry Blackaby's persistent and consistent challenge to every believer in response to practically any question was, and is, this:

"Find out what God is doing and join Him there!"

What is God doing in *your* business?

What is He doing in *your* community?

What is He doing in *your* industry?

Our advantage in knowing God gives us great benefit: We have an incredible opportunity to build the Kingdom of God and see God destroy the dirty deeds of the Devil. We have a unique opportunity to live a joyful, miraculous life every day. And we have a phenomenal opportunity to leave a legacy of wisdom for our family members and team members, so they can be, do, and have the life God created them to have, and in turn, leave a godly legacy of their own.

God's way is to *love* others! Love your team! Love your clients! Love your vendors! The Kingdom advantage happens when we allow God to love others *through* us!

---

1 Henry T. Blackaby and Richard Blackaby, *Spiritual Leadership: Moving People on to God's Agenda* (Seoul: Duranno, 2002).

Howard Partridge
International Business Coach
President, Phenomenal Products, Inc.
www.howardpartridge.com

CHAPTER 2

REDISCOVERING IDENTITY: ROOTING BUSINESS IN CHRIST

Dawn Sipley

"You need to ask for what you've earned, not what you think you deserve," declared Monica, her eyes locked on mine across the boardroom table. I froze in my tracks, my whole body flushed cold, yet my face was on fire, my eyes whelmed with tears. I had earned sweat equity in a company that I helped grow to $4 million, a business that had previously been in the red. Even though I was being groomed as the next CEO, I felt like something wasn't right, and Monica was urging me to discover what was lurking under the surface. My imposter syndrome was strong; I didn't feel worthy of my success. It kind of felt like it was luck, not my hard work, which had been the catalyst to my success. I still felt like the dirty little girl with the drug-addicted parents who embarrassed me in public.

I had asked for board advice through Seminole State College to help me navigate the transition, and Monica worked with them. I had areas of concern and was not getting support or clarity from my business partner, so I sought help. What came of that meeting was the discovery that I was being duped. My business partner was trying to change what we had rightly agreed upon. It wasn't what either of us felt I deserved. With my favorite verses in Matthew 20:1–16 deeply sewn into my heart, I knew the Holy Spirit had led me to this meeting with Monica. Jesus had spoken about workers in a vineyard then, and I was in the vineyard, and this was my parable about fairness and His unwavering love for us.

I had been a "parentified" child. Forced to grow up too fast and without adequate care emotionally or otherwise, I had found my worth in my ability to perform and achieve. Fiercely competitive and self-educating, I would go home each night to learn a new skill. I advanced my way from a part-time recruiter, earning fifteen dollars an hour, to an equity owner bringing in six figures annually—a dream for this little girl who had once been homeless. Even so, despite my success, I was empty inside.

My faith was constantly challenged in the workplace. I couldn't be as bold as Christ was calling me to be, so when Monica spoke, I felt broken. Was I disobeying God for someone who was taking advantage of my naïveté? My whole identity had been thrust into this organization, for which I felt a great deal of gratitude, but Christ was calling me to serve Him, not myself, and certainly not this man I was in business with.

With Monica's words playing in a loop in my mind and the boldness of Christ aiding me, I stopped being the "Yes Girl" I had always been and began to hold myself and others accountable. The result? A decade's worth of hard work seemingly crumbled in an instant when I received a simple email terminating my employment. Thankfully, it came during my church's twenty-one-day prayer time, and while I was still in the sanctuary. The jolt of this abrupt change served as a poignant reminder that I had let my ego inflate my sense of worth. While I had anticipated either a much-needed change or termination, I vastly underestimated the swiftness of the consequences. But God's timing is perfect.

During those twenty-one days, I found myself on my knees in the church, dedicating an hour each morning to prayer in alignment with my church family. During those moments, I had profound encounters with Jesus Christ, experiences that forever reshaped my life. Each evening, I spent an hour in quiet reflection, listening to God and capturing thoughts, ideas, and plans.

Remarkably, and without explicitly seeking it, a business plan took shape during these contemplative moments. I made a personal commitment to be still for an entire month to continue listening to His voice, as I embraced a period of curiosity. Given my childhood experiences, this was against everything that I found comforting. I just wanted to fix what I had broken. God led me into meaningful conversations, and I remained open to whatever introductions He saw fit to provide. Throughout that month, I kept an open mind and heart, allowing divine guidance to orchestrate the connections and opportunities that unfolded. This experience fundamentally transformed the course of my career and my life. It changed me at my very core.

After just one month of reflection, Sipley the Best was born with a simple Facebook announcement. I created a wild campaign for doing résumé writing for the ridiculous price of twenty dollars. I figured if I could make a hundred dollars a day for the short run, I could feed my family and have plenty of bandwidth left to build a company. My husband and I discussed it, and we agreed we would invest $30,000 in the creation of the business. If it didn't work within a certain time, we would pull the plug and blame the pandemic.

That following January I did a week-long fast for the first time. My vision and passion hit new heights; Jesus was my CEO. I reflected on my last twelve years of employment, and with counseling, was able to determine how my childhood had led me down the path I had been traveling for so long with such blinders on. I took accountability for my part, and slowly stopped finding my identity in how I performed. Instead, I woke up every day with a genuine interest in people. I was no longer compromising my ideals to please a man or my ego. Now I lived to glorify God with no boundaries. What a difference!

I had no idea how to start a business, but through my community connections, I plugged it together piece by piece, sharing my faith and testimony on an international stage. The business plan God built during my church's twenty-one days of prayer came to fruition. After the amazing response to my keynote speech on how our childhood trauma and neglect impacts our careers, I decided to write a book. Through my healing process and sharing, I have been able to meet people who have had their own forms of parental neglect. Whether it's a little boy who experienced the loss of his mother at the age of thirteen after a six-year battle with cancer, or the eldest daughter of a family in poverty who cared for her younger siblings daily, or the child of divorce who had to become the emotional support to the parent who was grieving after a deep betrayal, our childhood trauma doesn't clock out when we clock in.

Sipley the Best has grown consistently every year, now employing a staff of diverse backgrounds working in accordance with God's vision. Once I rooted my business in Christ and stood boldly in my faith, my pain and identity were forever changed. He was healing me. I am so blessed to live in a nation where I can exercise my faith boldly in marketplace ministry. Human resources infused with biblical principles build the most profitable and fruitful industry. I have met some of the most influential people of my life through my Central Florida Christian Chamber membership.

Doing business with other believers is a priority for me. Iron sharpens iron. I will forever be thankful for the intercessory prayer and the biblical mentorship I receive. I feel blessed to be able to live my calling in every area of my life—my business, my family, and my church.

My business is rooted in Christ, and the yoke has never been so light!

Dawn Sipley
International Speaker
www.sipleythebest.com

CHAPTER 3

CHRIST-CENTERED FOUNDATIONS: BUILDING ENTERPRISES ON ETERNAL VALUES

Ford Taylor

When I travel around the world, I ask this question: Who is the greatest leader of all time? I get the same answer in almost every city and in every country. It does not matter what level of faith, or what area of faith—Christian and otherwise—the hearers share, the answer is almost always, Jesus. So, I ask the next question: If Jesus is considered the greatest leader of all time, even if you didn't believe He was the Son of God (and I do believe that), why would I *not* use His leadership model to run my business, family, or any other organization? Why is that? When we ask what qualities and skills are desired in a leader, we get the same answers too. Interestingly, many of those named are exactly what Jesus had.

People want leaders that are visionary, caring, good communicators, humble, consistent, and decisive; good delegators as well as initiators with an understanding of the difference; good listeners, enthusiastic, and transparent; and possessing a good sense of humor. In Christian environments, they'll make that same list, and add traits like peaceful, patient, and kind, as well as exhibiting goodness, gentleness, and self-control, even longsuffering, along with love, meekness, grace, and mercy. So, if those are the qualities and skills in which Jesus walked, why would we not want to walk in those same attributes?

My question to leaders is this: What are we willing to do that others may not be willing to do to become that kind of leader? We take a look at the definition of leadership, and the definition I prefer is my own: "A transformational leader is willing to lay down their life for those whom they lead or influence."[2] I think it's clear that that's what Jesus did. Now with those attributes and with that definition, what is the purpose of leadership? What can we put in the foundation of our companies and organizations to be sure that we can grow and expand, and do it profitably, while lowering turnover and making our people happy? Well, the term I use is called V.S.T.T.E.E.L.E.

What Is V.S.T.T.E.E.L.E.?

The **V** stands for **Vision**. Leaders cast vision. An organization needs a clearly identified, practical, implementable, motivational, and compelling vision that people are inspired to follow.

The **S** equals **Serve**. After the vision has been cast, it is the leader's responsibility to serve and to see to it that the followers are taught, trained, and equipped so they are empowered to accomplish their roles in fulfilling the shared vision.

The **T** equals **Teach**. Leaders are responsible for providing knowledge that the followers need to perform their roles in moving the organization toward the vision.

The next **T** is for **Train**. Leaders must train their followers, which means providing them with the experience they need to perform, before fully giving them the responsibility to do it.

The **E** stands for **Equip**. To equip is to provide the tools necessary for your followers to perform at the highest level.

Before we move forward, let me clarify the difference between teaching, training, and equipping team members. Teaching provides new knowledge. Training provides experience. Equipping provides the actual tools to perform. For example, let's say you want your people to be taught, trained, and equipped on how to use a smartphone as well as multiple smartphone applications. If you brought them into a room and showed video presentations and distributed manuals to

---

[2] Ford Taylor, *Relational Leadership: When Relationships Collide with Transactions: Practical Tools for Every Leader* (Houston, Texas: High Bridge Books, 2021).

show them how to use it, that would be teaching. If a smartphone were given to each person and they were allowed to practice what they were reading about in the manual and seeing during the presentation, that would be training. If, after all the teaching and training they were sent back to work with a smartphone, that would be equipping.

What's Left? (The Remainder of V.S.T.T.E.E.L.E.)

The second **E** in **V.S.T.T.E.E.L.E.** equals **Empower.** When the follower has the knowledge (teaching), experience (training), and tools (equipping) to succeed, they are fully empowered and ready to do the job. At times, we think we are empowering people when we're merely delegating tasks. However, if we empower people before we've taught, trained, and equipped them, we can get them and our organizations into trouble, so those others must come first.

The Difference between Empowerment and Delegation

Delegation is different from empowerment; it's a precursor to empowerment. Delegation is part of the teaching, training, and equipping. Let's assume I have a new administrative assistant. He or she comes to work on Monday morning, and I explain that one of their responsibilities is to handle my calendar. Then I tell them that this Thursday I have four people coming for lunch who will arrive at 11:30 a.m. I ask my new administrative assistant to bring in three pizzas—one meat, one veggie pizza, and one cheese, as well as soda for four people, and a couple of salads with ranch dressing. Then I provide the name and number of the pizza place I prefer. I just described the process of delegation.

What does empowerment look like? Let's turn the clock forward ninety days. Over this time period, I have taught, trained, and equipped this person to understand how to manage my calendar. On Monday morning, the person comes into my office and says, "I noticed that you have four people coming in for lunch. Are there any special dietary needs?" I thank them for checking, and soon after, my assistant tells me the lunch will be there at 11:30. That's what empowerment looks like.

Later, perhaps the assistant will tap on the door, stick his or her head in, and say, "By the way, if you had put on your calendar that there were no special dietary needs, I wouldn't have had to bother you." You see, the training can go both ways to help us perform our jobs more effectively. When the relationship is strong, this sort of two-way training can happen.

The **L** stands for **Let Go**. Once you have empowered the person who has the requisite knowledge, experience, and tools, you can confidently let go, and allow them to fulfill his or her responsibility, moving towards the common vision.

The final **E** equals **Evaluate**. At this point, the job of the leader is to evaluate the person's performance, in light of clearly defined expectations and the vision for the organization. It is important that they know and understand how they are doing in their roles in relation to the shared vision.

V.S.T.T.E.E.L.E. Reduces Stress!

Think about a time when you may have sent one of your team members to do something *before* that person was taught, trained, and equipped. It could have been your employee, your child, or someone else. How did that go? What was your stress level during that experience? Conversely, how about a time when you sent one of your team members to accomplish something only after you first taught, trained, and equipped that person for the task at hand? Which experience was more productive? Less stressful?

Based on the V.S.T.T.E.E.L.E. model, how would you rate the quality of your leadership today? Think about where you want to be as a leader. Are you a teacher, trainer, and equipper? Are you empowering? Have you been delegating before (or after) your people have been taught, trained, and equipped? If you've been delegating before the person is ready, you may be stressed, and your team member and his or her coworkers may also be stressed as a result.

As you lead, try using the V.S.T.T.E.E.L.E. model. When you engage this model, leadership becomes much easier and less stressful. Why? Because we are building teams around us that are empowered through what and how we've taught, trained, and equipped them. Cast a compelling **Vision. Serve. Teach. Train. Equip. Empower. Let go. Evaluate.** As a result, you will become a highly influential, transformational leader who balances the need for good relationships in your organization with the necessary transactions that propel the organization forward.

We all have influence. We might as well make it a positive one.

When an organization has a clear, practical, implementable, inspirational, and motivational vision, great things can happen. Jesus cast a clear vision. What did He do next? He served those whom He had influenced or led. How did He serve them? He did it through teaching, training, and equipping. He walked with them and delegated responsibilities to them. Delegation is not a dirty word unless we intend to delegate forever.

Remember, delegation is telling people what to do and how to do it, when to do it, where to do it, and who to do it with. But that is only part of the teaching, training, and equipping process. Once those are also done, we can move on to empower. When we empower, we all grow. We as leaders strengthen our capacity as individuals as we build others inside our organizations too. After we empower, we can let go because we've given people clear role clarity and job descriptions. They know what is expected of them. Then, our job becomes to evaluate our progress. Jesus was the greatest leader in history. He started with twelve (and was only successful with eleven of them). That gives me great hope. Jesus now has between 2.2 billion and 2.5 billion followers. Why not model our leadership after the greatest leader of all time?

Jesus cast His vision, served, taught, trained, equipped, empowered, let go, and evaluated. He left the power of the Holy Spirit to evaluate further. I encourage you to adopt His leadership style. Begin by asking yourself this: What can I do to become this kind of leader? That's the best place to begin.

In chapter twenty-two, I'm going to give you a couple of other tools to put in the foundation of your business that we are told over and over and are two of the top tools we take into organizations that give long lasting profitability and success. Those tools are called V.P.M.O.S.A and a conflict resolution tool called the Social Covenant.

Ford Taylor
Author, Keynote Speaker,
Founder of FSH Strategy Consultants and Transformational Leadership
www.transformlead.com

CHAPTER 4

LED BY THE SPIRIT

David Roznowski (Pastor Roz)

A man visited my business, and as we talked, he began to share some of his burdens with his family and health, opening up about his emotions. I don't know why, but people have always been drawn to me, and just open up, pouring out the deepest depths of their hearts. As I listened, I felt extreme compassion and care for this man, and the conversation concluded with the usual "I'll pray for you" statement as we were to go our separate ways. However, before I could take the first step, I clearly heard the Lord tell me to "pray for him now." Immediately my flesh began to make a case as to why I couldn't, wouldn't, even though I was fully able. *I'm really busy, he's really busy, he's not religious*, I thought, and on and on. Walking back to my work area, I began to feel an overwhelming sense of conviction because of my disobedience in not praying. After a grueling minute of trying to ignore the weight, I rushed back to find the man. He was gone. I ran into the parking lot, searching, but I had missed the opportunity. Tears flowed as remorse filled my heart. Right then, right there, I repented and pledged to God to *always be obedient* whenever God was leading me by His Holy Spirit to do something.

What causes us to reject or ignore the guidance of the Spirit? When we look at Scripture about being led by the Holy Spirit, we find that listening and being obedient to Him was never bad, but always good. The Israelites discovered the goodness of God's leading when He delivered them from the bondage of Egypt as they followed the cloud of smoke and pillar of fire (Exodus 13:21–22). That same Spirit led them throughout their entire forty-year journey in the desert to inherit the Promised Land.

> *"By day, the pillar of cloud did not fail to guide them on their path, nor the pillar of fire by night to shine on the way they were to take. You gave your good Spirit to instruct them."*
>
> (NEHEMIAH 9:19B–20A NIV)

Paul also experienced God's goodness when the Holy Spirit "course-corrected" his missionary journey:

> *"Paul and his companions traveled throughout the region of Phrygia and Galatia, having been kept by the Holy Spirit from preaching the word in the province of Asia. When they came to the border of Mysia, they tried to enter Bithynia, but the Spirit of Jesus would not allow them to. So, they passed by Mysia and went down to Troas."*
>
> (ACTS 16:6–8 NIV)

This simple act of obedience to the Holy Spirit would result in hundreds, if not thousands, of people coming to know Jesus and being filled with the Holy Spirit as well as the birth of many churches. It would also lead Paul to later write the powerful New Testament epistles that encourage and challenge us today—those to the Philippians and Thessalonians.

Any time men willfully submitted to the Holy Spirit's leading, God accomplished the miraculous: He told Abraham to leave his country (Genesis 12:1–8); sent Philip to the Ethiopian eunuch (Acts 8:26–40); and Peter to Cornelius (Acts 10). Surely Paul was thankful for Ananias's obedience to the Holy Spirit's leading (Acts 9:10–19).

However, sometimes in the moment it doesn't always seem that the Spirit has our best interest in mind. For instance, in the account of Paul's obedience to the Spirit, we also read about his imprisonment! Paul was persecuted verbally, flogged with a rod, and placed in the darkest high security cell with no hope of escape. Was this also God's leading of the Holy Spirit for Paul? Yes, it was. How else could Paul's faith become unwavering without such testing? How else could the miraculous breakout that ended with the jailer and his whole family being saved have ever occurred?

Jesus is our greatest example for radical and complete obedience to the Spirit's leading:

> *"Jesus, full of the Holy Spirit, left the Jordan and was led by the Spirit into the wilderness, where for forty days he was tempted by the devil. He ate nothing during those days, and at the end of them he was hungry."* (LUKE 4:1–2 NIV)

Many times, it's the following of the most difficult leadings of the Holy Spirit that allows God to accomplish the greatest work in and through us. It was Jesus's following of the Holy Spirit, God's will, and purpose that led Him to that desert temptation and testing. And it was the Holy Spirit that later led Jesus to be mocked, beaten, and crucified that we might have eternal life through Him. Thank You, Jesus, for Your obedience (Philippians 2:8).

If God allowed and required obedience to the leading of the Holy Spirit, rigorous testing, and "weakness" from His own Son, how much more of us? Some of the toughest business and life decisions with which we are faced will be prompted by the Spirit's leading. Even our salvation is affected by God's leading of the Holy Spirit. Jesus said this:

> *"No one can come to me unless the Father who sent me draws [leads, impels] them."*
> (JOHN 6:44A NIV, ADDITION MINE)

So, why do we resist the greatest things God has for us? Why do we fight tooth and nail against receiving forgiveness, the call of a beautiful relationship with the Father, and the best God has planned for us? The apostle Paul understood this fierce inward battle that wages between disobedience by the flesh and obedience to the Spirit.

> *"So, I say, walk by the Spirit, and you will not gratify the desires of the flesh. For the flesh desires what is contrary to the Spirit,*

and the Spirit what is contrary to the flesh. They are in conflict with each other, so that you are not to do whatever you want."

(GALATIANS 5:16–17 NIV)

How do we win this battle? The Bible is clear. Being filled with the Holy Spirit will lead you to follow the Holy Spirit. A filling of the Spirit comes at salvation and then is refueled daily through prayer, the Word, and worship. As we walk through life, we must continually crucify the flesh and desire what God desires, not what the flesh desires (Galatians 5:24). We must believe that God knows best and desires our best. We must trust Him, even when we do not understand, or cannot see the end result.

Every day, God is giving us simple promptings to follow the Holy Spirit's leading, just as He urged me to "pray for him now" so long ago. Many times, the Holy Spirit's leadings can be those major course corrections that lead us to great trials … and miracles. Just imagine the great things God could accomplish in our businesses, lives, and for the Kingdom worldwide, if we would overcome our flesh, listen to, and obey the Holy Spirit.

Let's take a moment today to weep and repent of those times when we ignored the Holy Spirit's leading and did it our way instead. Let us promise God that we will be more sensitive and obedient to the Holy Spirit's leading in the future, desiring His will and not our own.

Let's never miss an opportunity again.

"But when He the Spirit of truth, comes, He will guide you into all the truth" (John 16:13a NIV).

David Roznowski (Pastor Roz)
Pastor, Founder of West Ohio Christian Chamber of Commerce
wochristianchamber.com

CHAPTER 5

UNVEILING THE INTANGIBLES: INFUSING THE FRUITS OF THE SPIRIT INTO BUSINESS

Joy Capps

I'm ashamed to admit it, but I spent many decades focused on the wrong things in life and business. As a communications strategist and veteran copywriter with over thirty years working for corporations, agencies, and even my own LLC, I inadvertently embraced the "do whatever it takes" mentality to help clients build brand awareness, increase engagement, and boost the bottom line. Without realizing it, I found myself indoctrinated and adept at weaving subtle manipulation into every presentation, team interaction, communications strategy, and piece of content. Success quickly followed as I cluelessly became a naive pawn in the games others were playing. *Perhaps you can relate?*

Losing Sight of My Values

In a world where "everybody's doing it, so it must be okay," my original, guiding principles faded into the background. Thankfully, Proverbs 22:6 would hit home later in life, turning me into the unexpected poster child for "raising a child in the way to live life so when she grows old, she will not depart from it." Put the emphasis on *old*—because my employer, job, and career became my top priorities for decades while my relationship with God diminished.

As a preacher's kid with a deep Christian heritage, my career didn't start off that way. Years of working for manipulative bosses and self-focused clients "rewarded" me for going to great lengths to make them look good as they achieved their goals. It didn't help matters that many scoffed and insisted that "God has no place in business." Their reprimands prompted me to leave Jesus at the door on the way in, and over time, I forgot to pick Him up on the way out.

In turn, my strong work ethic found me agreeing to work ridiculously long hours, twisting the truth with wee bits of hype, and using sensationalism for marketing communications that helped achieve Key Performance Indicators, or KPIs. While I drew the line at anything that broke the law, "selling my soul" to get ahead led me to participate in distorted workplace practices.

Praying for the Wrong Favor

Ironically, I quietly sought God's strength behind the scenes to help me navigate the many incredible projects and people I supported. My intentions were good, but my actions were far from it because I lived in a warped reality that blurred together worldly goals with Christianity. (*Sound familiar?*)

My prayers unintentionally became twisted as I constantly asked God for favor with my clients and colleagues. *Everything* I did focused on making my clients happy; I went above and beyond in my efforts to help grow their bottom line. (Many years later, I finally understood that the favor I needed was from God, not other humans.)

Sucked in the vortex of worldly ambition with selfish motives at the forefront, I gained accolades, awards, promotions, and recognition. Yet, I didn't realize I was missing God's blessings. I had learned to compartmentalize God, only turning to Him to bless something after I'd already created it. Instead of being my go-to, He became my last resort, the afterthought I sought once I tried everything else.

Good News through Life-Changing Catalysts

Several events helped me see what I'd been missing as the years passed. From getting my foot reconstructed and not walking for nine months, to supporting a client who used Christianity as a hook to bilk people out of large sums of money, God used situations to get my attention and start changing how I helped others (and myself) show up in the marketplace.

He showed me that walking with Him in today's business world was indeed possible. For the first time, I understood how to do life and business in partnership *with* God while also connecting with customers ethically and authentically. These revelations helped me see the need for communications that aligned with Him, which led me to create a new Spirit-led framework.

A Fruitful Framework

My new approach, which I call "joyful copy" and "joyful communications," uses marketing communications best practices filtered through God's Word. Far from typical, this technique became my *modus operandi* as I covertly started integrating it into every project, presentation, and client interaction. The more I tested and implemented this God-first approach, the easier it became to take a stand in the marketplace. (Fast forward to today, and I'm overtly sharing this framework with any who will listen, especially Christian business leaders—like *you*!)

With over 31,000 verses in the Bible, I needed a way to streamline the filtering process. The Holy Spirit's guidance illuminated Galatians 5:22–23 (the fruits of the Spirit) and Philippians 4:8 (a believer's thought life). Here they are:

> *"But the Holy Spirit produces this kind of fruit in our lives: love, joy, peace, patience, kindness, goodness, faithfulness, gentleness, and self-control. There is no law against these things!"*
> (GALATIANS 5:22–23 NLT)
>
> *"And now, dear brothers and sisters, one final thing. Fix your thoughts on what is true, and honorable, and right, and pure, and lovely, and admirable. Think about things that are excellent and worthy of praise."* (PHILIPPIANS 4:8 NLT)

These three verses now serve as the compass for everything I think, say, create, and do—with or without me vocalizing it. Before sharing *anything*, I pause to filter my strategies, ideas, and words through the sixteen characteristics found in these verses. If anything looks or feels out of alignment or carries even a whiff of subtle hype or manipulation, it gets revised until it emulates these godly attributes.

Applying the Fruits of the Spirit in Business

You can use this framework, too. Leveraging the fruits of the Spirit in the workplace—especially your marcom—is a breeze when you follow these steps:

- **Request.** Invite the Holy Spirit into everything from the start.
- **Review.** Filter whatever you create through the sixteen Christian characteristics outlined in Galatians 5:22–23 and Philippians 4:8.
- **Revise.** Rewrite any sentence, phrase, or section that uses subtle hype or doesn't align with God's Word.
- **Remove.** Extract anything that uses twisted realities or creates a false need to take action.
- **Reject.** Occasionally, you may need to hit the reset button and start afresh.

For practical application, compare this framework to the tires on your car. You may drive along without problems for a long time until something throws your tires out of alignment. You may not feel it at first, but after a while, it becomes evident that something isn't quite right. After troubleshooting, a mechanic may recommend an alignment. However, sometimes, your tires are a lost cause, and you need to replace them. Out with the old, in with the new.

How you show up in business is similar to evaluating tires—only you do it daily. You can be sure that what you're putting out in the world is aligned with the fruits of the Spirit by consistently reviewing *everything* you think, say, create, and do.

Word to the Wise

In full disclosure, my human nature sometimes rears its head with quick-witted sarcasm or worldly-focused thoughts. It isn't uncommon for self-focused objectives to provide distractions through money, trends, innovations, experts, and more. Whenever that happens, I apply liberal amounts of "holy duct tape" by asking the Holy Spirit to forgive me, help me see what He sees, and put His *super* into my natural. Now, that's what I call the Ultimate Game-Changer.

Wherever you find yourself in this journey, let me encourage you to intentionally partner with Abba Father first, doing your best to mirror the fruits of the Spirit in everything. Doing so makes all the difference. Instead of blending in with the status quo, displaying authentic positive transformation is sure to make you stand out.

Want to take a deeper dive? Check out my book, *Joyful Copy: How to Show Up in the Marketplace Ethically and Authentically* (available through online retailers) and listen to *The Joyful Communications Podcast* for tips you can use. Or reach out to me.

Joy Capps
Author, Podcaster
www.joycapps.com

CHAPTER 6

MIRACULOUS MOMENTS IN BUSINESS: RECOGNIZING GOD'S HAND AT WORK

Morris Hartley

I often find myself acting as though God works only on the important things in my life. Yet truthfully, God is at work in *every* part of our lives, and He wants us to seek Him with every need and in every circumstance. One thing that I have learned during my fifty-five years on this earth is that God cares about it all, and He acts on our behalf in both the important and the small. I have observed that although God wants us to ask, He will act without us asking. And throughout my corporate work experience spanning more than three decades (much of that as a business owner), I have learned that God wants us to consult Him about our businesses too. Absolutely *nothing* is outside His loving care.

To give you some context, let me tell you a little about myself and H & H Products Company. My dad, Len Hartley, started the company, trusting in God every step of the way. He had grown up in the family beverage bottling business, so he had some experience and knowledge in the industry. In 1964, my dad obtained a loan for $200 so that he could start his own business, initially working from the side porch of the house he shared with his parents. Yes, $200! Now, almost sixty years later, the company provides beverage concentrates and liquid food products to thousands of foodservice outlets across the country and internationally. God has been good to us! I started working full-time for my dad in 1991, holding various positions of responsibility over a ten-year span. After ten years, I took the reins as president. Recently my son, Jimmy, joined me to become the third generation of Hartleys at H & H Products Company. Thankfully, I am blessed to have my dad still around to see all that God is doing and share his wealth of knowledge with us.

Over the years, God has provided for us through abundance, scarcity, and everything in between. He has also protected us at times by putting up a big stop sign, and saying, "No!" I could share hundreds of miraculous "God Stories" of our sixty-year history of God's goodness and provision in the company, but I am going to limit it to three.

Constructing a New Building

In 1971, my dad purchased some land on the northwest side of Orlando and began constructing a new building that was five thousand square feet in size. However, in the middle of construction, his two largest customers—Steak-n-Shake and Pepsi—decided to use another supplier. My dad sought God and received a blessing that was greater than anything he could have imagined. By the time the new building was completed, H & H was producing for two new customers: McDonald's and Disney World. Losing so much business could have been devastating, but my dad had faith and saw his company prosper. God provided!

COVID-19

None of us will ever forget the year 2020. As COVID-19 spread throughout the world, schools and businesses closed, hospitals were overrun, and life as we knew it changed forever. Much of the food service industry slowed to a halt. I remember my dad saying that he always considered our customer base diversified in that we serviced restaurants, schools, theme parks, cruise lines, bars, convenience stores, and jails. But in 2020, such diversification didn't seem to matter.

We worked frantically to see how our company could survive during that time. One idea that came to mind was manufacturing hand sanitizer. The FDA opened production to anyone who wanted to try it, so they published the formula. We started exploring this opportunity. Our sales team jumped into action, and in a matter of days had orders for dozens of truckloads of hand sanitizer. As with most decisions, we struggled with whether this was the right direction. I was in contact with a company that could sell me alcohol for hand sanitizer. Right before calling them, I lifted up a very abrupt and honest prayer. I looked upward and said, "God, I need Your help." Yep, that was my entire prayer. Not eloquent. Not quoting Scripture. Not even an "amen." Just a raw cry to God. I picked up the phone, and after discussing all the pertinent information, I wondered if this would be flammable. And if so, where would I store it? I asked the gentleman who was helping me, and he told me to "just treat it just like gasoline." Next, I called a customer who manufactured alcohol-based products and sought his advice. After asking me a few poignant questions, he suggested that we were not set up properly to handle this and could bring harm to our plant and people if we pursued it. As quickly as we started, we stopped. God answered my prayer with a strong "no!" That "no" saved us from calamity. Though 2020 remained a difficult year for the company, God protected us, and our faith remained strong.

Moving

Over the next couple of years, God worked miracles for H & H. In 2022, our company grew at such a rate that by 2023, our production facilities needed to expand; we required additional office space, and our warehouse had become woefully small. At the beginning of the year, I started searching for new offices, the easiest piece to move. Office space was also inexpensive, as many vacancies existed after COVID-19. I contacted a friend who was a commercial real estate broker, and he started searching. In the initial conversation, I mentioned that it would be ideal if he could find me an office space that was already furnished. He admitted it would be a difficult task. Nevertheless, he found the perfect location, and we began finalizing a deal. The tenant who was moving out informed us that his company was going completely remote, so if we wanted any of the furniture, we could have it. God provided all the furniture we needed, and it did not cost us a dime! Our next challenge was the limited warehouse capacity. Adding an additional building was not a feasible option at the time, so we looked at the possibility of renting a warehouse instead. We reviewed several options that would meet our needs. As it turned out, the least expensive building was the newest and best location we found. It was exactly what we needed! Once again, God provided.

In Conclusion

Over these sixty years, God has provided for (and protected us) many times and in many ways. He has given us wisdom and confirmation on decisions, big and small. I love the verse that closes the Gospel of John:

> *"Now there are also many other things that Jesus did. Were every one of them to be written, I suppose that the world itself could not contain the books that would be written."*
>
> (JOHN 21:25 ESV)

The story of H & H Products Company is just like that! I am truly grateful that God has given me the opportunity to see His hand move in so many ways for our good, and I look forward to the "God Stories" yet to come.

Now, what are your "God Stories"?

Morris Hartley
President, H & H Products Company
www.hhproductscompany.com

CHAPTER 7

CULTIVATING A GODLY WORKFORCE: BUILDING TEAMS ALIGNED WITH CHRIST'S VALUES

Virginia Grounds

What a difference it makes when the staff of a business are led by values that align with those taught by Jesus. I can attest to this truth from my experience with working in a secular environment as opposed to an environment led by a believer who not only shared his faith but taught it as well. Therefore, I know the difference between working for those of faith and those who are not believers.

It is because of the chairman of the board for a mortgage company where I worked that I am a believer today. I was a young woman in my twenties at the time. Many years have passed since then, but I will always remember this man offering Bible study in his office on Wednesday mornings. It was not mandatory, but I had been taught to be a good girl, so felt I should go to set an example. Little did I know the surprise God had for me.

During that time, I was miserable and didn't know why. One day a coworker pointed her finger at me and said, "God has you under conviction!" (This was after she asked what was wrong with me and I had no answer.) I remained in this state for a while, unable to throw off the heaviness pressing upon me, and I was miserable. One day I saw a book at the grocery store on end times being taught based on the book of Revelation. When I finished reading the book, there was a prayer at the end inviting the reader to receive Jesus as personal Savior. That was a defining moment for me. On my knees beside my bed, I prayed that prayer. Immediately, the weighty burden of conviction was lifted.

I knew at that moment I had changed. God filled me with a hunger for Him and His Word that has never diminished.

Years later, when I was no longer working for that company, I saw the same man, Doc Swalwell, the one that had been bold enough to offer Bible study in his office. I was so excited to tell him about the difference he and the study had made in my life. When I did, his response was, "Well, thank you, Virginia, but I thought you were already a believer!"

I tell this story to prove the importance of sharing our faith in the workplace with everyone—whether we think they have faith or not. Just because someone is a good person doesn't mean they have faith in Christ. You never know who is just waiting for the prayer that will lead them home to Jesus. So, how can we do this?

- Live your faith with integrity, not caving to the world's point of view that does not line up with what God says in His Word.
- If you are an executive with decision-making authority, be a spiritual leader by encouraging the believers in your business to be examples of how to live a godly life through their words and actions.
- Send messages of hope and encouragement to your staff or coworkers.
- Have an open-door policy for spiritual discussions.
- If allowed, offer Bible study on a volunteer basis. Who knows? You could be the one used by God to have influence in someone's life.
- Be strategic by making changes in the work environment that will pass to the next staff or customer. Prayerfully plan ahead for how this will be carried out.
- Pray for your staff and coworkers regularly.

I don't know what went into the plan for making a difference in the workplace of the mortgage company. But I know there was a plan. Mr. Swalwell spent hours studying to teach Bible study. Then, he offered the study in his office. He did this consistently—week after week. God used him to accomplish His purpose of leading others to Him as we were exposed to the Bible. At least one life was brought out of unbelief in the darkness and into the marvelous light of Christ by the leadership and example of bold faith in the workplace. I will be forever grateful for the chairman of the board, the bold coworker, and the Bible study that changed my life.

Because of a corporate leader sharing Christ in the workplace, God called me to serve Him in Christian leadership through ministry and work.

My prayer for this book is that it will empower the mindset of Christian leaders in the marketplace to be bold both in sharing their faith, and in reflecting a Christlike example for those who are part of their team in the workforce.

> *"If I then, your Lord and Teacher, have washed your feet, you also ought to wash one another's feet. For I have given you an example, that you also should do just as I have done to you."*
>
> (JOHN 13:14–15 ESV)

Virginia Grounds
Author, Founder/Publisher of
Breakthrough Christian Publishing
www.breakthroughchristianpublishing.com

CHAPTER 8

ETHICS, EXCELLENCE, AND BETRAYAL
Jim Subers

"It *is* personal. It's *not* just business."

As a younger man, I had the opportunity to buy a business from an apparently very successful man who also confessed his faith in Jesus. He and I met on a mission trip to Africa with a national missions' organization. Beginning with that trip, and then over several months afterward, he discussed the sale of his business with me. At the time, I was running a manufacturing operation based in Israel. We developed handheld solar-powered audio units, loaded them with Scripture, and distributed them around the world, primarily to non-literate and unreached peoples.

I loved my work and was not planning to leave, so in order to consider buying this man's business, there were a number of hurdles I would have to jump. Since this was going to be purely an investment, I had to make sure that being an absentee owner could even work. This man assured me that it could and committed to stay on for at least three years as the manager of the business. He put the numbers together for me, and I took them to my accountant and financial advisor for review. It looked promising. Then I worked with a bank to secure the necessary financing, even enlisting an investment from a good friend.

On the day we closed the deal, and after I got the keys, he looked at me and said, "Jim, if we run into any conflicts in this business arrangement, remember, *it's not personal, it's business.*" It seemed like an oddly-timed disclaimer on that day, but it was actually a major red flag that I wished I had seen earlier. Over the next few years, this man worked behind the scenes to run the business into the ground so he could move me out of it and take control himself. Over time, despite his excuses and varied explanations, it became clear that the numbers he had presented in the beginning were bogus. Reality began to sink in: I had been deceived and defrauded. I was angry. This guy had used the name of Jesus and his testimony to earn my confidence and steal from me. He was clearly not who he said he was.

As the consequences of his deception became more apparent, they affected me emotionally and physically. I had trouble sleeping. I could think of little else. I was carrying the distress of these circumstances in my countenance and body language, and my wife and kids knew something was wrong. I was angry—at this man, at myself, and even, angry with God to some degree. This man's deception and fraud eventually caused me to lose the business, creating financial hardship for me, my family—and my good friend who had invested with me.

Thankfully, this experience did not shipwreck my faith, for I already had a strong relationship with Jesus. However, when those who claim "faith in Jesus" act without integrity in their business dealings, it can destroy not only their own testimony, but also cause others to curse Christ and Christians. It has a ripple effect that can keep many from the Kingdom.

In Proverbs, Solomon says, "The Lord detests [hates] lying lips, but he delights in people who are trustworthy" (Proverbs 12:22 NIV, insertion mine). I began to detest this man for what he had done to me, my family, and my friend. Not only was I dealing with the practical results of his sins against me, but I was also dealing with my own sin—by harboring "hatred" in my heart toward him.

It has been said that hatred and unforgiveness is like drinking poison, and hoping it kills the other person. I recognized that I needed a deep work of forgiveness toward this man. Forgiveness did not mean I ever had to do business with him again, nor did it mean I could not seek legal action against him, but it did mean that I had to change the way his actions had affected me by changing the way I thought.

I determined that whenever he came to mind, I would confess under my breath, "I forgive him." Initially, I did this multiple times a day. Over time, I thought of him less and less. Now, he seldom comes to mind; and when he does, I am able to genuinely pray for God's blessing on his life. The Scripture is clear: "The integrity of the upright guides them, but the unfaithful are destroyed by their duplicity" (Proverbs 11:3b NIV). My hope and prayer for him is that he will come to a place of repentance and restoration.

Those of us who call on the name of Jesus are called to live to a higher standard. We have decided to reject the Kingdom of this world and we are set free from its control. God has made us "new creations," and we are no longer slaves to the old kingdom. We have a new King and new values, and we are subjects in a new Kingdom.

The old kingdom, the kingdom of this world, teaches that "it's not personal, it's just business." However, its values stand in direct opposition to the values of this new Kingdom and its King. The old kingdom says:

"Do whatever it takes to win."

"Bending the truth is okay, as long as you don't get caught."

"Appearance, not integrity, is paramount."

"The end justifies the means."

"Put yourself first."

"If it feels good, do it."

The new Kingdom says, "It is not just business, *it is personal.*"

"Do to others as you would have them do to you."

(LUKE 6:31 NIV)

"Because of my integrity you uphold me and set me in your presence forever."

(PSALM 41:12 NIV)

> *"Have a clear conscience and desire to live honorably in every way."* (HEBREWS 13:18B NIV)
>
> *"Keeping a clear conscience, so that those who speak maliciously against your good behavior in Christ may be ashamed of their slander."* (1 PETER 3:16 NIV)

Further, Paul tells us this:

> *"Do not be conformed to this world, but be transformed by the renewing of your mind. Then you will be able to test and approve what is the good, pleasing, and perfect will of God."* (ROMANS 12:2 NIV)
>
> *"You are not your own; you were bought at a price. Therefore, honor God with your bodies."* (1 CORINTHIANS 6:19B–20 NIV)

And in his letter to the Ephesians, he makes it clear that the way we do business and the way we live our lives needs to be decidedly different to the way the world does business. He says:

> *"Among you there must not be even a hint of sexual immorality, or of any kind of impurity, or of greed, because these are improper for God's holy people. Nor should there be obscenity, foolish talk, or coarse joking, which are out of place, but rather thanksgiving. For of this you can be sure: No immoral, impure, or greedy person—such a person is an idolater—has any inheritance in the Kingdom of Christ and of God. Let no one deceive you with empty words, for because of such things God's wrath comes on those who are disobedient. Therefore, do not be partners with them. For you were once darkness, but now you are light in the Lord. Live as children of light."* (EPHESIANS 5:3–8 NIV)

Jesus Himself said, "Let your light shine before others, that they may see your good deeds and glorify your Father in heaven" (Matthew 5:16 NIV).

God has placed each of us in our unique positions and given us a distinct network of relationships that we touch and influence. For many people in our network, we may be the closest example of a follower of Jesus that they will ever know. As a result, the responsibility we have to represent Jesus to them may have *eternal* consequences.

If we are to be salt and light in a culture enveloped in darkness, and if we are to glorify God with our lives, then the way we do business and the way we treat others must be decidedly different than the values promoted in the broader culture.

It is personal! It is *not* just business!

Jim Subers
CEO, Vision Orlando
www.visionorlando.org

CHAPTER 9

FROM LOCAL TO GLOBAL: THE TRANSFORMATIVE POWER OF KINGDOM THINKING AND ENTERPRISE

William A. Snell Jr.

I recall Jesus saying, "These things I have spoken to you so that in Me you may have peace. In the world you have tribulation, but take courage; I have overcome the world" (John 16:33 NASB).

Trouble is like running into the Devil and realizing that if you don't confront your arch enemy from time to time, you might be heading in the same direction.

Our journeys of personal growth and transformation are often accompanied by spiritual opposition. As others have done, you too can learn to use the weapons of spiritual warfare that Christ Himself commissioned and walk more intentionally in life under the guidance of the Spirit. Remember the words of Christ that we just read: "Take courage; I have overcome the world." The pace of societal change can be dizzying. What once took a century to achieve can now be accomplished in a matter of months. This rapid transformation can be alarming, especially for those of us who see the decay of our Judeo-Christian culture advancing unobstructed.

Yet, for those with eyes to see and ears to hear, Christians have an advantage over those outside a personal relationship with Jesus Christ. Operating in an environment where love, forgiveness, purpose, grace, and favor flow in abundance can be a life-changing experience. It can help us to grow, learn, and become better versions of ourselves. When we are surrounded by love, we feel supported and encouraged. Forgiveness allows us to let go of past hurts and move forward with a renewed sense of hope. Purpose gives us direction and meaning, while grace reminds us that we are all human and that we all make mistakes. Finally, favor is a reminder that good things can happen to us, even when we don't expect them. Together, these elements create a powerful dynamic that can help us live our best lives before God while making a positive impact on the world around us.

Sounds like transformative success to me!

Those who do not reside in the Kingdom environment mentioned earlier will weather anxiety and worry by resorting to self-help techniques, manipulation, or blame, which can lead to increased levels of intolerance and irritation toward others. Philippians 4:6–7 encourages believers to overcome anxiety and instead place their faith and confidence in God—who loves, cares, and provides.

I have come to realize that anxiety and worry occasionally visit everyone, but frequent (or repetitive) seasons of anxiety, care, and concern can become debilitating and destructive to all things valuable and worthy of time and effort. These troublesome traits have a toxic nature about them, serving to deplete creative thinking while paralyzing important decision-making. If left unchecked, worry and anxiety can become an infectious disease hindering personal growth and development, as well as economic advancement. However, developing spiritual insight and skills to overcome anxiety more effectively are essential for surviving in a competitive, and often antagonistic, environment and are also crucial for thriving and making an enduring impact in life.

"If God is for us, who can ever be against us?"

(ROMANS 8:31 NLT)

The fact is that many will be against you, and they will do what they can to diminish, perhaps even poison, what you have and what you stand for. Envy and jealousy can be powerful motivators for those who are intimately familiar with anxiety and worry. The truth is that God is on your side, and no matter what weapon is formed against you, He is bigger than it, and His resources will never be depleted on your behalf.

> *"Why are you cast down, O my soul? And why are you disquieted within me? Hope in God, for I shall yet praise Him for the help of His countenance."* (Psalm 42:5 NKJV)

Please heed my advice. Stop worrying! Put an end to repetitive anxiety! You can do this! The Holy Spirit can and will empower you to comprehend what is true and what isn't, and He will lead you into truth and nothing but the truth. The result? Your mind will be liberated. Truth will set you free, and where the Spirit of the Lord is, there is freedom![3]

Lies and deception create an atmosphere of worry and anxiety, often leading to mental and social prisons. Instead, we can transform our minds by practicing Philippians 4:8:

> *"Finally, brothers, whatever is true, whatever is honorable, whatever is just, whatever is pure, whatever is lovely, whatever is commendable, if there is any excellence, if there is anything worthy of praise, think about these things."* (Philippians 4:8 ESV)

Otherwise, if left unchecked, these strongholds of defeat and fear will take root in relationships, business, and family. However, by employing faith and hope, recognizing that you "can do all things through Christ who strengthens" you, you can experience joy, freedom, and renewed confidence (Philippians 4:13 NKJV). This alone will make a significant difference in your home, office, and place of ministry.

"Stop worrying. But seek first the Kingdom of God and His righteousness."[4]

---

3   See 2 Corinthians 3:17.
4   See Matthew 6:25–34.

What do we know about the Kingdom of God and God's ways? We know that God's ways are not like ours, which are often influenced by earthly, sensual, temporal, and insecure desires for power and prestige. However, the principles of God's Kingdom, which is the environment of His rule and reign, work to our benefit every minute of every day—even through hardship, rejection, and failure. In fact, God uses much of what serves to dismantle the efforts of others to equip, mature, and advance us toward Christlikeness and transformative impact as Romans 8:28 says.

The apostle Paul illustrates this as he confronted the conventional wisdom of his day, saying, "Most gladly, therefore, I will rather boast about my weaknesses, so that the power of Christ may dwell in me ... for when I am weak, then I am strong" (2 Corinthians 12:9b, 10b NASB).

Greater influence and success must come through the crucible of weakness and failure. For most, there is no other way of advancement. Those who choose to comprehend and embrace the rule and reign of God, learn to admit, and embrace, their weakness. Contrary to what the world says and believes about humility and self-disclosure, you will be more loved and admired as a result, and trust from others will increase, not diminish.

During the first three years of my tenure at Missionary Ventures International (MVI), my daily commute was about ninety minutes each way. Although it was expensive due to gas prices, wear and tear on the automobile, and toll roads, the lengthy drive proved to be providential. As the weight of the ministry settled upon me, I found myself increasingly anxious and worried. Money needed to be raised, staff needed to be encouraged and better equipped, and cultures and languages were confusing and intimidating. These made me increasingly insecure.

If it weren't for my ninety-minute commute—during which I could air out my concerns before the Lord—I doubt that I would have been as successful in overcoming my negative thoughts. On one occasion, my anxiety reached its peak, and I was still an hour away from the office. Amid great despair and futility, I sensed the Lord break through to my heart and mind. Although it may not have been audible, I heard Him clearly:

"Billy boy (the endearing name my deceased father often used), I did not call you to fail. I've got this!"

God lovingly intervened in my life when I was struggling with anxiety, fear of failure, and worry. Although I knew better than to let these feelings control me, the fact is that I had been weakened over time and had grown increasingly insecure, unable to break free on my own.

There was a time I seriously considered passing the leadership baton to someone else. I'm glad I didn't because when my Father spoke to me in His loving and comforting way that day, I was healed, delivered, and set free to live and lead above worry and anxiety. In time, God showed me and others how "He had this." Today, MVI is meaningfully involved in 107 countries, registering thousands of churches planted, with more than 1 million salvations yearly through gifts of transportation made possible by our ministry partnership with the Christian Motorcyclists Association.

Whatever you are facing today, whatever your weakness or failure, be reminded that "He has this!" Better yet, He has you!

Stop worrying! Seek first the Kingdom of God, and His righteousness, and everything else will follow.

William (Bill) Snell Jr.
President, Missionary Ventures International
www.mvi.org

CHAPTER 10

NAVIGATING MODERN MARKETS WITH ANCIENT WISDOM: 1 CORINTHIANS 3, A BIBLICAL BLUEPRINT FOR KINGDOM COMMERCE

Krystal Parker

Let's time-travel back to Corinth, circa 55 AD. The city was an economic powerhouse with a kaleidoscope of cultures and beliefs. Imagine wandering through the bustling streets. Breathe the air rich with the scent of the sea, exotic spices, and freshly baked bread from the market stalls. Picture New York in the ancient world strategically placed between two significant ports, a natural hub for land and sea trade. This is Corinth, a thriving commercial hub, not unlike the competitive marketplace you navigate every day.

Corinth was the Silicon Valley of its day—a place of innovation, wealth, and cultural diversity. The marketplaces were filled with traders from across the globe, selling everything from luxurious fabrics to priceless pottery. Temples to gods like Aphrodite and Apollo stood proudly, reflecting the prevailing polytheistic culture.

This was the backdrop against which the early Christians lived, and it wasn't easy. Trying to keep their faith strong in a city that celebrated everything in opposition to their values and beliefs was a daily challenge.

That struggle continues today. While our nation's roots are deeply entwined with faith-based principles, our modern society embraces an increasingly diverse array of beliefs and viewpoints. It's an evolution that mirrors the cultural tapestry of ancient Corinth. In today's business landscape, as a business owner and Christian, you must navigate a complex environment where a multitude of worldviews coexist. How do you be a standard-bearer for your faith in a marketplace that often diverges from a biblical worldview? Balancing these dynamics requires not only business acumen but also spiritual wisdom. How do you keep your faith at the forefront while driving your business forward?

Billy Graham said, "One of the next great moves of God is going to be through the believers in the marketplace." The marketplace is where faith meets action. At a time when traditional church attendance has waned, the role of Christian business leaders in sharing the gospel is even more crucial. Their daily interactions in the business world provide unique opportunities to advance the Kingdom of God, as the early Christians in the city of Corinth discovered.

Our businesses are more than a livelihood; they are a platform for impact. Every transaction, every interaction, is an opportunity to embody Christian values, much like the early Corinthians who navigated their faith amidst a thriving anti-biblical worldview economy.

Paul's letter to the Corinthians is not just ancient Scripture; it's a strategic guide for Christians in the business world—then, now, and for the future.

1. **Identity in Christ.** "We are only God's servants through whom you believed the Good News" (1 Corinthians 3:5 NLT). This identity in Christ is crucial in business. It guides our decisions and interactions and helps us maintain integrity as we function against diverse worldviews. It's a compass for Christian leaders, keeping them grounded in their values and purpose.

2. **Foundation on Jesus Christ.** "For no one can lay any foundation other than the one we already have—Jesus Christ" (1 Corinthians 3:11 NLT). In business, this foundation supports every decision, ensuring that our practices reflect our

faith, which is especially crucial in a world where integrity is often challenged by prevailing business norms.

3. **Role of the Holy Spirit.** "For the wisdom of this world is foolishness in God's sight" (1 Corinthians 3:19 NIV). In the whirlwind of entrepreneurship, the Holy Spirit provides wisdom and discernment, guiding business decisions and helping to navigate the complexities of the modern marketplace.

4. **Community and unity.** "God's temple is sacred, and you together are that temple" (1 Corinthians 3:17 NIV). Paul knew the power of unity. He called the Corinthians worldly as there was jealousy and quarreling among them. He addressed divisions in Corinth, emphasizing the importance of unity. In business, this translates to fostering collaboration, respect, and a shared vision, essential for a successful and impactful Christian enterprise.

5. **Coworkers in God's service.** "For we are coworkers in God's service; you are God's field, God's building" (1 Corinthians 3:9 NIV). Ministry goes beyond the four walls of the church. Paul tells us that business is a tool for ministry, often called "business try" or "business as mission" (BAM). Christian leaders in the marketplace have unique opportunities to impact and witness, reaching more people than can be done in traditional church settings.

As business owners at the crossroads of faith and commerce in a rapidly changing world, the teachings of Paul in 1 Corinthians 3 are as relevant and vital as ever. While the setting of ancient Corinth was different, the principles outlined in this blueprint hold true now more than ever. They remind us of our identity in Christ, our foundation on Jesus Christ, the role of the Holy Spirit, the importance of community and unity, and our responsibility as coworkers in God's service. These teachings challenge us to run our businesses on principles that go beyond profit.

Embracing this ancient wisdom, we apply it not only as a strategy for success but also as a commitment to transform our world through our work. Our businesses are more than profit-making machines; they're platforms for changing lives and advancing God's Kingdom.

Aren't you glad the early Christians had the courage to keep the gospel moving through the marketplace? Their steadfastness laid the groundwork for our faith today. It's our turn to carry the banner. With the wisdom of 1 Corinthians 3 as our guide, we can continue this legacy of faith-driven entrepreneurship.

Krystal Parker
President, U.S. Christian Chamber of Commerce
www.uschristianchamber.com

CHAPTER 11

REFINER'S FIRE: SANCTIFICATION BY OBEDIENCE ... OR DISOBEDIENCE

Simon Bois

Raised in a broken home, poverty hit Mom and I hard after my parents' divorce. That was followed by some turbulent teen years during which I made some pretty bad choices. Eventually, I found myself panhandling my way back to a home I could not afford to rent. Then God…

Born in French-speaking Quebec, Canada, where less than 1 percent of the population is of the Protestant faith, my parents and family (with the exception of one uncle and aunt) were far from practicing the Christian faith. With a functioning alcoholic hard-working mom who eventually passed due to cancer, and a promiscuous artistic dad who took his own life, I was an only child, left to figure out life by myself. To be fair, Mom and Dad were never truly dealt a great hand of cards in life from the start. They did the best they could knowing what they knew.

When I was seven, two Gideon missionaries witnessed to my parents in my presence. Both Mom and Dad were stone cold, and the Gideons did not realize that I was paying close attention to the message of Christ. That message resonated within me—deep down in my core. I felt irresistibly drawn and called.

> *"My sheep hear my voice, and I know them, and they follow me."* (JOHN 10:27 KJV)

The "following" part was the challenging piece. I went home with Mom and Dad that day, reading the Gideon's New Testament, and signed the salvation prayer in the back of it. I was filled with hope. How could a seven-year-old boy be supported and encouraged in his new walk of faith? My dad's side of the family was heavily involved in occult sciences. My mother's side could not care less, except for my grandmother, who was a devout Catholic. Need I explain the manifestations and hostile spiritual oppression I experienced?

My teens hit me quick and hard. I grew hurt. Hurt was all I knew, so I did not realize the hurt I was living with. Compounding my woundedness was anger. I was deeply angry to a depth that surprised me later. I am not looking for pity here. Just stating facts. I did not know there was a life outside of hurt, anger, and betrayal. I was surviving. Despite that, and looking back, I can see God's hand at work in my life, putting the right people and circumstances in my path.

One of them was a Christian camp called Camp Brochet in northern Quebec. It was the only camp Mom could afford. For only ninety-five dollars, Mom was offered the opportunity to farm me out for two weeks—lodged and fed. A nice yearly break for my mother. Little did she know I would be fed, yes, but not only with physical food. I was also fed spiritually. The Gideons' gospel message was echoed every summer through this camp. It built foundations in my heart that I desperately needed. Each year I came back renewed and on my best behavior for my mother. Each year my youth and immaturity made sure this behavior was short-lived. Without support or mentoring, I was left to myself. My good old anger and hurt would rear their ugly heads in my heart and lead me into bad—very bad decisions—over and over again. The party life was the only way I could numb my pain. It was a vicious cycle, and I soon found myself addicted to numbing the pain in whatever ways I could. Fill in the blank here if you will.

In my early twenties I was driven to make a life for myself. As best as I could, I took opportunities to feed my entrepreneurial spirit. School? Nah. Why bother? Armed with a high school diploma, I decided to face life successfully and learn the only way I truly enjoyed learning—hands-on. Additionally, I had learned that I could not part ways from my Bible. Even if I went seasons without reading it, I made sure it was with me at all times—and in proximity, no matter where or when. I looked at it like it was a lifesaving device. Books were my go-to source of wisdom when I needed to figure things out. When facing challenges, I always read all I could on a topic to achieve my goals.

My early to late twenties were stormy, to say the least. The consequences of my bad choices as a teen led me to living below the poverty level on the streets of Toronto, Canada, for a short time. One glorious, divine night, I found myself broke, broken, and without a job. I wept at the realization that my life was spinning out of control—and fast. Something had to change, or it was not going to end well. Sitting alone on the floor of my unaffordable "furniture less" room, I gazed through my mess and there it was—my faithful Bible.

Staring right back at me, it was calling me. I knew this was my only salvation. "But God," I said, "I always let You down and I don't want to let You down again!" God's response? No voice was heard, but thoughts of wisdom were planted in my heart from Him: *I will never let you down. Ever. All I ask is that you come to Me and trust Me in good times—and especially in bad times.* At that very moment, an unspeakable peace overcame me. *Tomorrow, I want you to go to that little church you always walk by—Bethel Baptist Church on Dundas Road—and speak with the pastor. Then put your life in My hands.*

French-speaking, I could barely manage a sentence in English, but I obeyed. The morning I met with Pastor John Freel rather unconventionally, we spoke at length. He and the whole congregation embraced me, encouraged me, and mentored me. One good brother, James Baird, patiently took my calls as early as three in the morning as I wrestled to understand the Bible. Because I was unable to master the English language well enough, I was also unable to get jobs that were up to the measure of what I felt were my great entrepreneurial talents. I was humbled to scrubbing toilets at a Super Fitness gym part time. Every decision, every choice, every thought, every action, every reflection about anything in my life from that point on was submitted to what the Scriptures taught. Literally. No one had ever taught me the meaning of honor, ethics, integrity, hope, love, kindness, forgiveness, and the list went on. Every day I would eat up Scriptures, absorb its teachings, and apply the values I discovered in them. Naturally, being exposed to English writings and fellowshipping in English rapidly improved my command of the language. God crowned my heart with an insatiable curiosity—the desire to learn and to create. He satisfied me through His Word, specifically Proverbs. Every day for years, I read the chapter of the corresponding date over and over again. That helped me grow so much and turned out to be a pivotal maneuver of my God in blessing me. That is, personally and professionally.

My journey lifted me progressively: from begging on the streets of Toronto to scrubbing toilets to survive, to temporary administration work available because of my growing grasp of English. In time, I took on more significant roles and responsibilities in public relations in the transportation branch of the provincial government in Ontario (MTO), eventually becoming an assistant to elected representatives in not one, but two, different (and opposing) administrations. I was on top of the world (at least I thought I was)—but then God. He was not done with me!

I crossed paths with a book entitled *What Color Is Your Parachute?* by Richard N. Bolles. I believe from his writing that he is a man of faith as well. Here's an excerpt from the cover:

> *For more than fifty years,* What Color Is Your Parachute? *has transformed the way people think about job hunting. Whether searching for that first position, recovering from a layoff, or dreaming of a career change,* What Color Is Your Parachute?

has shown millions of readers how to network effectively, compose impressive resumes and cover letters, interview with confidence, and negotiate the best possible salary—while discovering how to make their livelihood part of authentic living.[5]

God put this book in my reach because He knew I had dreams that I did not even know I had! He was not about to let my dormant entrepreneurial gifts rot in my present governmental administrative environment. That book changed the direction of my life. God combined the ideas from the book with His Word, and the result propelled my career to new levels I never thought possible. I guess you can say God helped me get rid of the red tape!

By choice—and with many "growing pains," I eventually became a sales consultant to a small Canadian corporation that did about $2 million in annual revenues. My role was to market their products in a $6 billion vertical market. I worked with the heavy-duty transport equipment market of semi-trailers, branding private and common fleets in Canada first, and the U.S., second. Today, this client, Turbo Images Inc., has become one of the top five in their market, enjoying in excess of $20 million in business in mainland North America. As pretentious as this will sound, I need to point out that $10 million of that $20 million was the direct result of my efforts, but I could not have accomplished that without God and the people He put behind me. Naturally, my role grew, and I eventually became the Sales VP. Three other clients, one British, one American, and one Canadian, benefited from my journey with God, as I helped them successfully penetrate the North American market. This showered me with accolades, but I give the credit to God. My clients know where I stand. I don't preach. I mention my faith in God in a timely fashion using tactful diplomacy, and if someone wants to know more, I gladly share. I remember on several occasions when calls or even cold calls naturally

---

[5] Richard N. Bolles, *What Color Is Your Parachute?*, accessed January 23, 2024, https://parachutebook.com/.

progressed into joint times of prayer. More importantly, I act on the values the Bible taught me; I execute, and I deliver, equipped with God as my Ally.

As if all that were not enough, God has also blessed me with the privilege to be published in a domain I simply love—the motorsport industry, since 2001, in both the U.S. and Canada, and in both French and English. This opportunity has opened doors for me to interview highly successful and influential individuals, using this platform to inspire my readers to reflect on their lives, values, dreams, and all the invisible—and sacred—parts of our existence. Prominent injury attorney Fran Haasch and her husband Rhett Jones in Florida have taken notice of my work and supported my endeavors faithfully. I will forever be thankful for them.

Sadly, I paid dearly on a personal level for my selfish pursuit of professional goals. The hurt of my early days was still deeply rooted and unhealed there. After fourteen years of marriage, and with a beautiful home and three precious children born in the U.S.A., I had to come to grips with the result of blindly following my own selfish ambition and pride. In 2018, God allowed my marriage to dissolve. The divorce was messy and hostile, to say the least, leaving a great deal of pain in everyone's hearts. This taught me that personal spiritual growth, and not professional success, should always be priority number one—especially at home. It is a delicate and challenging balance to maintain. There is more to that part of the story as I am still learning, but that might be for another literary project.

Obviously, I have made many grave errors in my life, and continue to fall prey to pride and selfishness on a daily basis, but I will always give glory to my God for my children, the abundance of blessings He has infused into my heart, my soul, my spirit, and my life. Every hardship and failure has truly become a blessing for which I am thankful today. I will likely fall again, but my anchor is rooted in the Word of God:

> *"For the righteous falls seven times and rises again, but the wicked stumble in times of calamity."*
>
> (Proverbs 24:16 ESV)
>
> *"If I speak in the tongues of men or of angels, but do not have love, I am only a resounding gong or a clanging cymbal. If I have the gift of prophecy and can fathom all mysteries and all knowledge, and if I have a faith that can move mountains, but do not have love, I am nothing. If I give all I possess to the poor and give over my body to hardship that I may boast, but do not have love, I gain nothing. Love is patient, love is kind. It does not envy, it does not boast, it is not proud. It does not dishonor others, it is not self-seeking, it is not easily angered, it keeps no record of wrongs. Love does not delight in evil but rejoices with the truth. It always protects, always trusts, always hopes, always perseveres. Love never fails."* (1 Corinthians 13:1–8a NIV)

What now? I am focusing on blessing my children, and others (including my clients), with my gifts, and doing my best to elevate them. I intend to let go and let God continue to sanctify me. My advice to you? Work hard. Play hard. Yes. Be sure to "clean your room," as Dr. Jordan Peterson would say in his amazing work entitled *12 Rules for Life: An Antidote to Chaos*.

Simon Bois a.k.a. "Florida Night Train"
Author, Senior Executive Corporate Director
www.facebook.com/FloridaNightTrain

CHAPTER 12

INTEGRATING WORSHIP: THE ROLE OF PRAISE AND PRAYER IN BUSINESS

Dr. Joshua Steinke

"I know what your problem is. You have Musical Tourette's Syndrome!" I'll never forget that accusation. As if "Musical Tourette's" was a real thing. "What do you mean?" I said laughingly. "Every time I walk by, you're singing a different song. Out of nowhere you just start singing aloud!" said the accuser. We both laughed, and then I took the opportunity to explain.

It's true that I'm guilty of singing often and singing loud. It's not about making noise or music; it's not for the attention or because I'm even that good at singing. It's certainly not because I get paid to do it.

The reason for this seemingly sporadic behavior could be summed up in the refrain of that old hymn written by Civilla Durfee Martin, "His Eye Is on the Sparrow":

> *"I sing because I'm happy, I sing because I'm free,*
> *For His eye is on the sparrow, and I know He watches me."*

You can find the culprit of my condition throughout the text of Psalm 150. "Let everything that hath breath praise the Lord. Praise ye the Lord" (Psalm 150:6 KJV). The words written in Ephesians 5:19 I have taken quite literally: "Speaking to yourselves in psalms and hymns and spiritual songs, singing and making melody in your heart to the Lord" (KJV).

Perhaps the most interesting side of this "condition" is that God has called me to be a business owner. Not just a business owner, but a doctor in a busy practice who sees upwards of hundreds of patients on a given day. Therefore, a lot is at risk regarding reputation, income, patient satisfaction, and online reviews. Considering all of that, I remain completely convinced that those words in Ephesians 5:19 and Psalm 150 aren't really a suggestion, but a command for any blood-bought, redeemed and restored, saved-from-the-grips-of-hell, Holy Spirit-filled believer. If we wake up with breath in our lungs today, if we are thankful for what the Lord has done in our lives, and if we have the opportunity, then we should PRAISE THE LORD.

I truly do not believe there should be a separation between work and worship. After twelve years of running a small business, I am convinced that one of the most effective and powerful ways to encourage people, break down walls, and evangelize the community is through praise and worship throughout the workplace.

When someone walks into my office, the first thing they hear is worship filling the waiting room. The next thing they most likely hear is singing from one of the doctors, or the office staff laughing at one of the doctors singing. You see, the joy of the Lord accompanies praise! Again and again, we hear people make statements like, "There's just something different about this place. Just walking into the office, I already begin to feel better." That may seem like a strange statement, but I believe it's the presence of the Holy Spirit that is welcomed daily to inhabit our business, and it is largely due to ongoing praise and thanksgiving. I have witnessed day after day how worship music inside of our work environment has softened the hardest men, has drawn people to ask questions about my faith, has encouraged someone through the lyrics they hear, or has allowed a stressed-out mother to take a deep breath.

Music alone doesn't do a whole lot (even when it's Jesus' smusic). There must be something deeper. That's where people come in. When we take music and couple it with a transformed vessel (you and me), then we get praise. If you add thanksgiving and prayer to the recipe, then your result is an environment where the Spirit of the Lord is transforming lives. Who doesn't want that in their business?

It doesn't have to be singing. Maybe you can't carry a tune in a bucket. Maybe the cats cover their ears when you try to belt out "Amazing Grace" in the shower. While I still believe you should sing with all you have to the Lord, it may legit scare some business away. In that case, find another way to integrate worship into your business. Timbrels and dance, the harp, the lyre ... something! The bottom line is that our praise and worship in business should be an undeniable reflection of our restored life in Jesus.

Equally important to workplace praise and worship is prayer. One of my pet peeves in our current social-media-heavy world is the comment, "I'm praying for you," without any sincere follow through. It's become as cliché as saying, "Good to see you." Sometimes you mean it; more often you don't. Therefore, we've personally made it a point to pray when we say that we are going to ... not eventually, but immediately. I have found that if I don't pray on the spot for someone who needs it, then I will quickly forget to. Since we know the power and importance of prayer, it is so important that we follow through with it. Since day one of opening our small business, I have made it a point to pray before, during, and after our business hours. We pray in our business, around our business, for our business, and with our business. I can't tell you the amount of people who have said these words over the years: "I wish there were more businesses that prayed for their clients like I've experienced here." Certainly, we don't pat ourselves on the back here. We have many things we can improve upon, but my observation has been that it absolutely changes outcomes when we pray in business (and not just a little).

What would it look like if every Kingdom-minded business intentionally made praise and prayer a part of their day-to-day culture? What if the sound resonating through the walls of every Christian workplace was about the life-changing message of the gospel, the goodness of God, and our hope in Jesus? What would it look like to walk into your barbershop, the health food store, the coffee bar, or the ice cream parlor and know that the people there could and would pray for you at any given moment? We can change the culture around us, especially through our businesses, by simply "singing because we're happy, singing because we're free."

I'll leave you with one last story. Years ago, a well-to-do businessman found himself lying on one of our chiropractic adjusting tables in Room #2 (that seems to be the room where all the miraculous things happen). When I walked into the room, he was lying face-down. I began to ask him about his woes when he suddenly interrupted me and asked, "Is this worship music playing above my head?" I replied with a simple, "Yes, it is. It's all we listen to here, actually." His response was direct, "You know, it isn't 'my thing' but I can't deny that it's peaceful. There's something different about this place." After I finished adjusting him, I proceeded to pray for him, his healing, and his family. He looked me in the eye before leaving and said, "I've never had anyone do that before. I'll be back." That man sent several of his workers and friends to our office over the years. He gave monetarily to many of our philanthropy and ministry events, but never attended one of them. He helped us to spread the gospel in our community without ever seeing it. I often think how different that outcome would have been if we had kept our praise and prayer to ourselves.

Dr. Joshua Steinke
Chiropractor, Director, Worship Anyway
www.worshipanyway.com
www.Ohiofamilychiropractic.com

CHAPTER 13

THAT THEY MAY BE ONE: THE POWER OF KINGDOM COLLABORATION

Jim & Martha Brangenberg

"That they all may be one; just as You, Father, are in Me and I in You, that they also may be one in Us, so that the world may believe [without any doubt] that You sent Me."

(JOHN 17:21 AMP)

Collaboration: noun: To work together, especially in a joint intellectual effort.[6]

When you encounter the living God, it changes you. When you *follow* the living God, it benefits everyone around you—whether they believe in Jesus or not. To pursue Christ is to pursue the same things He did: love, justice, peace, truth, healing, unity. These characteristics are what set Christians apart from the rest of the world. In fact, Jesus said, "By this everyone will know that you are My disciples, if you have love and unselfish concern for one another" (John 13:35 AMP). So, what do you think happens when pre-believers see believers fighting, competing, and arguing amongst themselves?

It doesn't make our faith attractive, that's for sure.

Did you know that there are roughly 45,000 denominations globally?[7] If we focus on the United States, there are over 200

---

[6] "Collaboration," The Free Dictionary, accessed January 14, 2024, https://www.thefreedictionary.com/collaboration.

[7] Gina Zurlo, Todd M. Johnson, and Peter Crossing, "Status of Global Christianity, 2024, in the Context of 1900 –2050," gordonconwell.edu, accessed January 14, 2024, https://www.gordonconwell.edu/wp-content/uploads/sites/13/2024/01/Status-of-Global-Christianity-2024.pdf.

denominations, 330,000 Protestant churches, and 3,000–4,000 ministries exclusively focused on discipling workplace believers. Since the birth of iWork4Him in 2012, my wife, Martha, and I have talked with over 10,000 people and thousands of active organizations within the Faith and Work Movement. Through our podcasts and events, we've had countless discussions with individuals who've had their lives radically transformed by the realization that their work matters to God. Hallelujah! However, many of those rooted in a business background want to develop their own curriculum, study, or round table to disciple other workplace missionaries instead of utilizing what already exists.

In other words, there are a whole lot of Christian groups with similar missions but separate budgets, buildings, employees, and fundraising. This rash of overlapping, but separate, ministries should make us pause and consider a few questions, such as: Where is all the unity that Jesus prayed for in John 17:21? When we focus on individuality, what kind of message are we sending to an unbelieving world about *who* we are, and more importantly, *Whose* we are? Imagine the Kingdom impact we might have if we gave up *competing* with one another and *collaborated* with one another instead!

In 2019, Martha and I were contemplating the direction of iWork4Him, and I distinctly remember praying, "Lord, I want to be a collaborative Kingdom leader. If You just show me what *real* Kingdom collaboration looks like, I'll reproduce it." I don't recall exactly how I got the answer, but I know that the Holy Spirit convicted me immediately: I had been praying for the wrong thing. Instead of waiting to be *shown* Kingdom collaboration, God was asking me and Martha to *practice* Kingdom collaboration, so that others could witness and replicate it.

At the time, I didn't know exactly what Kingdom collaboration looked like, but I'd seen plenty of collaboration in business, so theoretically, I was familiar with the idea. In business, collaboration was about working together toward a common goal or purpose with a willingness to lay down the chance for individual accolades or credit. Collaboration in the working world looked like group projects, business partnerships, and joint ventures. However, when you added the Kingdom- prefix to *collaboration*, something fundamentally changed. Now you are not collaborating through human power for human aims; now you are collaborating with God's power for God's aims. Kingdom collaboration is about setting aside individual identities and agendas in favor of selflessly serving together in pursuit of God's goals.

When the people of God work together for the purposes of God, impossible things can be accomplished.

Imagine this scenario: Twelve ministries in the same geographic area are all focused on reaching workplace believers. Despite their common mission, each ministry has a unique niche or area of discipleship on which they focus, and each ministry regularly encounters people who would probably fit one of the other eleven ministries better. If we practiced Kingdom collaboration, we would be actively referring those who are not the best fit for our ministry to one that's a better fit for them.

Kingdom collaboration means letting go of pride. Kingdom collaboration means placing the interests of others above the interests of self. Kingdom collaboration means getting rid of a scarcity mentality. There is no competition in the Kingdom of God, only a clear, concise commission assigned to everyone. The Kingdom collaboration concept echoes Jesus's heart in John 13:35 and John 17:21, when He said that our unity as believers would serve as a living testimony to a world aching for something to believe in. We would not be building *our ministry,* but instead devote all our energy and resources to serving His Kingdom overall.

So, let me ask you: Are you a Kingdom collaborator? What actions are you taking to foster partnership in your city, industry, or sphere of influence? How are you contributing to collaboration within the body of Christ? Are you among those who have initiated their own endeavors, and are engaging in competition within the body? Alternatively, are you someone ready to relinquish personal ambition and identity for the collective benefit of those around you—whether they need to encounter Jesus for the first time or deepen their knowledge of Him?

As Christians, each of us is a single thread within a great tapestry. Each has a unique calling, but our unchanging corporate purpose is to make disciples of all people. It's this purpose that weaves us together in unity. It is in this collaborative tapestry that the world is able to see the face of Jesus. So, I beg you, never view another brother or sister in Christ as a competitor. Instead, try to see them as co-laborers.

If you feel the Holy Spirit tugging on your heart to disciple workplace believers, I encourage you to do so with the heart of a Kingdom collaborator. As the body of Christ, there are countless ways we can assist, develop, pray, offer feedback, or partner with one another. If you aspire to be a collaborative Kingdom leader in an existing role or are considering a new and potentially groundbreaking endeavor, I invite you to connect with us at iWork4Him.com/contact. We can help you find individuals and ministries that align with the vision God has placed on your heart! We also offer support through prayer as you discern God's direction. Together, let's foster Kingdom collaboration and explore the transformative journey that lies ahead.

Remember, when we work together with God and one another, we can accomplish far more than we could alone! So, let us unite in Kingdom collaboration to reach all workplace believers with the good news that their work matters to God and that they have already been assigned a place of ministry: their workplace mission field.

Jim and Martha Brangenberg
Co-Founders iWork4Him
www.iWork4Him.com

CHAPTER 14

DIVINE APPOINTMENTS: SEIZING GOD'S ORDAINED OPPORTUNITIES

Dana A. Dunmyer

How do you go from being a pastor to the founder and president of a technology company with client footprints in 110 countries? Well, it wasn't my idea. I had no clue, no blueprint, no roadmap, no GPS. I only knew in my heart that God wanted me to have nothing to do with mediocrity, with preaching to the choir, or pretending the established church was as successful as we see in the New Testament. I knew from the time I accepted Christ as my Savior that I would not, could not, be a waste of skin. I had to do something that would honor God in every way. I had to be a part of the God I read about—not the one stuck in a shoebox somewhere and brought out when it was convenient or opportunistic.

I was indeed called to be a pastor when I was sixteen. It was about six months after I came to know Christ. After diverse preparation, I was called to serve Christ in churches as a pastor in Pennsylvania, greater Chicago, Michigan, Florida, and California. I was called to be the Compassionate Ministries Director of Operation Andrew: Hurricane Relief Ministry for our denomination. I was recognized as a successful pastor and had all kinds of growth recognition achievements and powerful experiences. I made sure we were paying our denominational apportionments for the general church, the district church, as well as our universities, compassion ministries, and missionary budgets. I was being groomed to be a denominational leader. The problem was this: I felt conflicted. My beliefs didn't line up with what

I was doing and seeing around me in the church. There is a disconnect that occurs when your beliefs don't line up with your actions. It's an uncomfortable state of mind when someone has contradictory values, attitudes, or perspectives about the same thing. It's called cognitive dissonance. However, I knew God is so much bigger, so much more loving, and so much more powerful than what was being accepted by the church as a whole.

God had called me to have faith in Him and His purpose for my life. I needed to commit my life's work to the God who loved and saved me. He deserved my very best. I had to live a life that would make a difference for His Kingdom. I knew God called me to this.

Just as I was called to be a pastor, I was equally called to resign my church in southern California and trust God and follow Him on a faith journey—one foot in front of another, trying to be sensitive to the Holy Spirit's leading. This meant more conflict though, because my wife and I had been raised to believe that if you are called to be a pastor and you do anything else instead, you are turning your back on God and "He would punish us for that." Nonetheless, we started a journey that led me, my wife, and two daughters to lose much of what we had owned, get emotionally and mentally ground into the dirt and homeless for a time, eventually finding a *sleazy* (underscore that word three times so you can imagine its impact) one-room hotel near Cincinnati in which we lived for many months. To be perfectly vulnerable, I turned into an orange. I was absolutely worthless for a while. I couldn't believe how I had so totally failed God and screwed up our lives so badly—just to go on this "faith journey" of mind. My wife, Connie, and daughter, Sarah, were much stronger and helped me through it.

As we were trying to figure out how to correct life, Connie and I both signed up with Kelly Services. It was a starting point and all we knew to do. At that time, Connie was called to a company as a temp doing forecast analysis for a call center. It was 1995 and I received a call from GE Aircraft Engines (now GE Aerospace) looking "for someone who knew something about this new Internet thing." I said I could do it. It's a long story, but my experience started with an AOL chat room.

I was thrown into the middle of a project tying in the Department of Defense, the Federal Aviation Administration, and GE's Quality Systems Group. I was the only "worker bee" but was surrounded by a few VPs and general managers to whom I reported my progress and needs. After about three months, I felt God's thumb in my back, urging me to have a meeting with the president. I also asked one of the VPs for a meeting with him. I was just a dumb preacher boy, so I had no idea how ludicrous my request was. I gained favor with the VP, and he got me a five-minute meeting, telling me to take only four and a half minutes because the president didn't understand technology anyway. He didn't even have a computer. His email was printed by his secretary; he scribbled a response on paper, and she sent it for him.

Two and a half weeks later, I got the meeting. I presented what I knew. It was a three-point sermon that went like this: 1) Here's where we are using the Internet. 2) Here's where I believe we can go using the Internet. 3) For some reason, I believe I am supposed to be the one that takes you there. After that, I gave him an altar call that went like this: A) Hire me as a C-Level and I will lead this thing for GE and answer directly to you. B) If you don't like that option, then permit me to start my own company and I'll lead GE in this venture. Or C) If you don't like either of these options, then I'm going to take this to Proctor & Gamble next door. I know they would love to have this.

He turned that five-minute meeting into about an hour and a half and ended it by telling the VP that arranged it to drop what he was doing, escort me to Columbus, and help me get the new company paperwork completed with all the details necessary for that. He ended with, "Do it tomorrow. Dana's company is going to lead us on the Internet."

There is so much more to this story. We sold off our first company in the dot-com days in an IPO (Initial Public Offering). We started several others. We celebrated twenty-eight years with GE last year, and today, we are serving God as "equippers of the saints" in technology ministry with over ninety-five products, bundles, and services that God paid us to create *for such a time as this*.

Our faith journey confronted mediocre expectations and comfortable assumptions. God used an ordinary family—one easy to overlook. God has rewarded our faith and obedience and made us into world changers.

Dana Dunmyer
President and CEO of TQI Solutions
www.tqi.solutions.com

CHAPTER 15

STRENGTHENING SPIRITUAL BONDS: THE HEART OF CHRISTIAN COLLABORATION

Nicole L. Davis, PhD

Jesus said that a house divided against itself cannot stand (Matthew 12:25). A house can be represented by a kingdom, a city, a community, a family, a business, or a church.

Any seemingly healthy goals for sustainable growth in any of these groupings are an illusion unless they include an intentional and deliberate focus on building up the individual member.

Furthermore, the ties that bind these inhabitants together may only be holding things in place by a mere thread. For Christians, our biggest determiners of success cannot be based solely on the size of our staff, the square footage of our facilities, or the bottom line. We need to carefully gauge the degree of our spiritual influence and how people feel when they encounter us.

There are two organizations that have been the most influential in my Christian life: the military and the local church. Both organizations have allowed me to flourish in my knowledge of God and my service to others, while building confidence in my professional abilities too. However, one organization, the church, also sought to stifle my confidence and the extent of my service to conform to their preconceived notions of the role of women in the Kingdom of God.

When I was twenty years old, I was invited to attend a Bible study in a singles' fellowship group nearby. In Keflavik, Iceland. I was interested but nervous. I was a young Navy girl who had never been to a Bible study before. In fact, I didn't even own a Bible! Since I didn't think I would know anyone other than the person who invited me, I too invited a friend to go along for additional support. I had no idea what I was getting myself into, and I didn't want to do it alone.

When I arrived, I was immediately welcomed with friendly faces. There were members from all military branches present—different ranks, backgrounds, socioeconomic statuses, ages, ethnicities, and denominations. However, they were all together that night for the sole purpose of spiritually strengthening one another in the Word. I was surprised to recognize some familiar faces I had seen around the base. This immediately put me at ease.

One encounter at that study would change the course of my life forever. An elderly man from the Air Force approached me and asked if I had accepted Jesus Christ as my savior. I said no, to which he responded, "Would you like to?" He prayed the prayer of salvation with me, and that evening I walked out of that meeting as a newly saved Christian!

For many months after, I went to Bible study any chance I could to continue to grow in faith with my new brothers and sisters. Being among them made me feel like I really *could* do all things like Philippians 4:13 said! Everywhere there were men, there were women also—whether it was serving in leadership positions, teaching, or praying. Regardless of who you were, they encouraged you in your talents to further the Kingdom of God. We were all equals; each of us was one of God's many children.

After years of service, my husband and I were honorably discharged and moved back to the States. I was heavily involved in our local church and acquired several ordination titles, including one as a minister. Some years later, we were looking for a new church, and decided to join one that had exceptional youth programs for our two sons. I gradually became more involved and accepted a leadership role, but this came with stipulations that were in stark contrast to what I had experienced in the military.

At this new church, they refused to recognize any of my ordination titles, as they taught that women could not be pastors, and I was not allowed to be called by the same title as any male leaders in the church at that time. This felt personally disrespectful and eroded my trust in the sincerity of their support of my efforts. This often led to disputes and divisions between me and some of the men on the leadership team. For a church with so many members and resources, I couldn't understand why we weren't taking advantage of them to their full capabilities. I often felt siloed in my leadership without adequate assistance.

I later learned that many of the men had been taught that women should not hold leadership positions at all, so it was difficult for them to accept the value that I and many other women were trying to bring to the organization. Apparently, all they could see was our gender. For this reason, many women have felt marginalized, undervalued, and overlooked in the church. Until men and women see themselves as spiritual equals, there can be no collaboration to build the Kingdom as completely as we should be doing.

This delay of Christian collaboration is not limited to men versus women either. In fact, it's nothing new. In Paul's letter to the city of Galatia, he addressed a similar issue between the New Jewish Christian converts and the Gentile Christians. The Jews were taught that they were God's chosen people, and were therefore, special. They were brought up under cultural traditions to which they religiously adhered, and which they thought were of paramount importance to follow God properly. As a result, they couldn't see how the Gentile Christians could also be partakers of Christ's salvation *without following their rules*. However, Paul's letter revealed that it was not their traditions that saved them, but freedom and grace through Jesus Christ. They were seeing it as a cultural matter when they should have been seeing it as a spiritual one.

Many organizations—unfortunately, churches included—commonly operate in culturally-focused work environments, ones in which rules, practices, traditions, and perceptions dictate how things will operate. Decisions are made from the top down with little use of consultants or feedback. As Christians, we should cultivate a spiritually-focused work environment—one where the Spirit leads instead. The shift starts with us. We must believe that if God can *save* anyone, He can also *use* anyone! Paul summed it up best in Galatians 3.

> *"For you are all sons of God through faith in Christ Jesus. For as many of you as were baptized into Christ have put on Christ. There is neither Jew nor Greek, there is neither slave nor free, there is neither male nor female; for you are all one in Christ Jesus. And if you are Christ's, then you are Abraham's seed, and heirs according to the promise."*
>
> (GALATIANS 3:26–29 NKJV)

This is what I first saw in the military. When we truly see one another for his or her spiritual gifts, we all work better together and achieve greater things for the glory of God. Our unity in spirit produces oneness in ability. That is the heart of Christian collaboration.

Nicole L. Davis, PhD
Co-Founder of Empower to Engage
www.empowertoengage.com
www.evewhereareyou.com

CHAPTER 16

TRANSFORMATIVE BUSINESS PRACTICES: CRAFTING A KINGDOM PARADIGM FOR SUCCESS

Robert Fukui

In 2022, I was in my mid-thirties and had a thriving career in marketing and sales for a Fortune 100 company. I had been married to my childhood sweetheart for five years, and we had recently purchased our first home and bought a puppy. She too had a growing career.

By all signs, we were a young couple achieving the American dream and enjoying success.

A week before Christmas, I kissed my wife goodbye, gave her a hug, and pulled out of the driveway, so that she could back her car out of our tandem driveway. I watched her drive away, not knowing it would be the last time I would see her alive.

Literally ten minutes down the road from our home, she got into a car accident and died at the scene. I didn't find out until that evening when I came home to find the Los Angeles County Coroner at my doorstep to tell me the news.

In an instant, my world was turned upside down, and everything I thought was important—wasn't. All my to-do lists, sales quotas, investment accounts, and meetings had no meaning. My definition of success was being challenged, and so too, would be my way of doing business.

The World's Definition of Success

We live in a society that defines success by hard work and accomplishments. In fact, many times hard work is admired more than the quality of our relationships. This is ingrained into us from a young age. My dad placed a great emphasis on getting good grades and working hard. The value of relationships was never a topic of discussion.

Society teaches us that in order to achieve success—whether it be in our career or business, we must work hard and make personal sacrifices. The thinking goes like this: *The sacrifices you make for your business today will benefit your family later. So, they'll understand.*

We justify not being present in exchange for professional and monetary success, thinking our relationships will take care of themselves. Let's pause for a moment. Do you really think your family wants your *presents*? No, they want your *presence*.

The Kingdom Definition of Success

Having a thriving business is important for sure, but not at the expense of your family and other vital relationships. That's not God's definition of success.

In fact, it's through relationships that we are able to discover, and achieve, true success. We begin with our relationship with our heavenly Father, then our family, and our friends and colleagues.

In Genesis, God created man to steward (or work) in the garden and have relationship with Him. God later created woman because God said, "It is not good that the man should be alone" (Genesis 2:18 ESV).

As illustrated, work is part of our calling, but true Kingdom success is only realized when every facet of our life—our faith, our family, *and* our finances (or business)—are in proper alignment and healthy. Are you succeeding in all three of these three areas?

The World's Best Practices

Many entrepreneurs start their businesses under faulty assumptions, best practices, and mindsets. Thought leaders warn startups not to expect much of a life or salary for the first three years of launching their business.

So, what do they do? They work long hours, sacrifice their personal life and time with family for very little pay, hoping for the pot of gold at the end of the rainbow.

Proverbs 23:7 says this: "For as he thinketh in his heart, so is he" (KJV). What you focus on will be what's attracted to you. If you think that long hours and lack of personal time is what it takes to be successful in business, you will live that out. A self-fulfilling prophecy.

In fact, early in my consulting career, I fell into this same trap. I thought "busy" was what I needed to be in order to grow my business so two a.m. bedtimes were common. By the time the weekend came, I was "spending time" with my current wife, Kay Lee (seventeen years by God's grace), but was mentally and emotionally checked out. I was exhausted. This wasn't sustainable.

Following the world's "best practices" to *succeed* with its primary focus on business alone leaves little time for anything else. It drives a person to a place where they find themselves saying, "I don't have time for (fill in the blank)," and no longer really living. I had to make a change.

Kingdom Best Practices

Working long hours and neglecting Kay Lee wasn't God's best. Yes, I wanted to build a successful business, but I wasn't going to sacrifice my marriage in the process. My new definition of success had to be measured by the health of my relationship with God, my wife, and then business. So, I started with these relationships first. That has made all the difference. I believe that if you focus on your relationships, you can still make a lot of money. But if you focus on money, your relationships will suffer.

The only way to have it all is to focus on relationships first. When you honor God (and family) with your best, He'll bless the rest. That's Kingdom.

More Time Can Kill

While the world thinks working more hours is what it takes, God says otherwise. If you haven't noticed yet, He's big on rest.

God rested on the seventh day of creation. One of the Ten Commandments is to obey the Sabbath. Jesus was often caught resting. In fact, the Bible's emphasis on rest is not just for our spiritual benefit. It's for our physical, mental, and emotional health as well.

Back in 1986, *Science* magazine published a research article on heart disease. It noted that the most common time for a heart attack was around nine a.m.[8] Why? The body needs time to acclimate to the vertical state after resting in a horizontal state all night. So, rushing into the day, checking texts, emails, then off to work, is stressful on your heart.

Further, the World Health Organization published a report in 2021 that found a 35% increase in heart attacks in people that worked more than thirty-five to forty hours a week.[9] It also said that "between 2000 and 2016, the number of deaths from heart disease due to working long hours increased by 42%, and from stroke by 19%."

More Time Decreases Productivity

Henry Ford conducted his own research in his factory, and showed there was no difference in productivity between the employees that worked forty hours per week and those that worked fifty. Economist John Pencavel from Stanford University published a productivity study with similar findings to Ford's. His study found that there was no difference in outcome between those that worked fifty hours weekly and those that worked seventy hours weekly.[10]

---

8   Gina Kolata, "Heart Attacks at 9:00 a.m. | Science," Science.org, July 25, 1986, https://www.science.org/doi/10.1126/science.3726536.

9   "Long Working Hours Increasing Deaths from Heart Disease and Stroke: Who, Ilo," World Health Organization, accessed January 24, 2024, https://www.who.int/news/item/17-05-2021-long-working-hours-increasing-deaths-from-heart-disease-and-stroke-who-ilo.

10 John Pencavel, "EconPapers: The Productivity of Working Hours," EconPa-

In summary, working longer hours provides no additional benefit, yet increases your health risk, lowers your productivity, and negatively impacts your personal time and relationships. There's simply no benefit.

Create More Margin

For true Kingdom success, you need to prioritize your relationships. Then you will become more efficient and productive in your business. How do you do that? *Increase your margin of time and money.*

Time

As business owners, we (I include myself on this list too), waste more time than we care to admit. When I say waste, I'm not just referring to checking social media or browsing on the Internet aimlessly or even playing games on your phone. I'm specifically talking about engaging in tasks *below our pay grade.*

Should checking emails, sending out invoices, putting out fires, and other various administrative duties be handled by you? The more time you are focused on those kinds of tasks, the less time you have for the more important Big Picture innovations necessary to move your business forward. And it's those plans you *enjoy most* as well. They should be a priority.

For me, it's developing content (like this chapter) that will benefit entrepreneurs. It's building strategic relationships and taking the time for long-range planning. Too often I put these things off to tend to more immediate needs—the endless stream of mail I should lay aside—and of course, the urgent and necessary too. I must align my work with my goals and delegate.

In Exodus 18:13–26, Moses's father-in-law, Jethro, paid a visit and observed how handling all of the Israelites' issues consumed Moses's time. A line a mile long formed that day—a line of problems

---

pers, accessed January 24, 2024, https://econpapers.repec.org/RePEc: iza: izadps: dp8129.

and disputes—and Moses handled every one of them. At the end of the day, Jethro admonished Moses, warning that he would wear himself out. Jethro proceeded to counsel Moses into establishing a leadership team to handle the Israelite problems. That way he would only handle the most difficult issues. Moses listened.

In order for you to be a more effective leader, accomplish more, move the business forward, and have a life, you need to *get stuff off your plate*. Just like Moses.

In general, we tend to fill our day by handling low priority items first because they are the current "need," relatively quick to handle, and provide immediate results. The higher priority items can easily fall into the background of our day. They take time and usually bear fruit slowly, so even though those long-range plans, for example, are vital to the future of the business, they don't realize immediate results. As a result, they're easy to put off. Hence, a lack of growth.

Roadblocks to growth start at the top. I've found this to be true in my own business and in those of our clients. The more tasks we control, the less things get done. So, begin with you. Take the time to assess how you are spending your office time. Look around you and be sure you are delegating, and not micromanaging. Ask God for His direction as you build a strong team.

Money

Many times, when a business is struggling financially or trying to get to that next phase of growth, they think more sales is the answer. It can be part of the answer, but it's not usually the entire solution. In fact, adding more sales to an already overworked staff can be detrimental.

The root issue for their financial woes is usually a lack of profit margin. According to a study by New York University, the average net profit margin across all businesses and industries is 7.7%.[11] Most

---

11 Controllers Council, "Controller/CFO Kpis: Net Profit Margin," Controllers Council, May 8, 2023, https://controllerscouncil.org/controller-cfo-kpis-

CFOs and controllers would say 10% is good, 15% is healthy, and 20% is ideal.

When a business is operating with lower than "good" profit margins, it forces them to work longer hours since their low margin won't allow them to hire more help. So, they try to achieve more sales, more customers, and more volume. If your business is already busy, what does *more* do for you?

In most cases, it's simply *more stress*. In fact, *more* can do more harm than good.

In order to improve your financial situation, alleviate some pressure, and put yourself in a position to hire more help or resources to improve the business in the future, you need to increase your profit margins. This is done in three ways: raise prices, decrease costs, or execute a combination of the two.

Raise Prices

This is the easiest thing you can do to increase profits, but it's also the hardest to implement. Therefore, it's often overlooked. The fear of raising prices and losing customers is common.

The best way to address this is with a simple word problem.

Let's say you sell women's clothing, and you have a pair of jeans that cost $99 wholesale and you sell them for $100. How many units to you need to sell to achieve $50 in profit? Fifty.

OK, so if you decide to sell that same pair of jeans for $149—instead of $100, now how many units do you need to sell to achieve $50 in profit? One.

Will you lose customers at the higher price? Maybe. But who cares? You don't need *all* the customers—just the *right one*.

---

net-profit-margin/#: ~: text=According%20to%20a%20study%20from,a%20strong%20net%20profit%20margin.

Decrease Costs

Decreasing costs is not necessarily slashing budgets. It's about increasing productivity and return for the money you're investing in the business.

Take labor costs, for example. Henry Ford slashed labor costs, not by firing people, but by increasing their productivity. He streamlined production (through some early automation) in such an efficient way that it cut the production time of a chassis from five days to one. This lowered labor cost/chassis cost by 80 percent![12]

That increased the company's margins so much that Ford was able to lower the price of his cars while doubling the wages of his employees. For the first time, the average consumer could purchase a car. Demand catapulted.

Ford transformed the industry. That's Kingdom!

A Combination of Both

In most cases, it's the combination of raising prices *and* lowering cost at the same time that will lead to the increased profit margin considered healthy for your business.

When was the last time you evaluated your financial statements with a fine-tooth comb and questioned everything? "Know well the condition of your flocks" (Proverbs 27:23 ESV). It's not enough to know you have sheep; their health is important too. So, inspecting how everything is doing periodically is vital to the bottom line.

Money or profit is not the most important for your business, but it is necessary for the long-term health of the business, and ultimately, the impact it makes for the Kingdom.

---

12 "Company Timeline," Ford Corporate, accessed January 24, 2024, https://corporate.ford.com/about/history/company-timeline.html.

A Call to Action

Success in the Kingdom is holistic. It's not focused solely on money or achievements but has a much wider range than that. God's version of success covers your overall well-being.

You can succeed in every facet of your life—faith, family, and finances—simultaneously, but that begins with a renewed mindset. A change in focus. It's time to stop accepting the world's standards and adopt God's instead. With God, all things are possible.

Prioritize your walk with God and your important relationships first. This still leaves you with more than enough time to build a Kingdom business.

Give God your best! He'll bless the rest.

Robert Fukui
Marketing Executive, Author,
Co-Founder Power Couples by Design
Website: https://marriedentrepreneur.com

CHAPTER 17

MISSION-DRIVEN VENTURES: ALIGNING BUSINESS GOALS WITH HEAVENLY PURPOSE

Craig Hohnberger

I was with Clarke, a business client of mine, at his favorite steakhouse, celebrating the fact that Jesus had become my Lord and Savior just a few days earlier.

As I thanked him for his witness and fervent prayers, he said, "I have something to thank you for, Craig: I am no longer the third servant." As a brand-new believer, I did not know much about the Bible at all yet, so I was puzzled, and it must have shown.

Clarke showed me where to find the parable of the talents in Matthew 25:14–30. He had me read it aloud. He explained that the Master of the estate represents Jesus, the servants represent us, and the darkness is hell. He also shared that while the word "talent" actually translates to "money," he believed it could represent so much more.

After all, God, knowing the English language would eventually dominate the world, including the global economy, may very well have intentionally chosen that particular word. In English, it could also refer to our actual talents, experiences, relationships, businesses—and any other resources we accumulated.

My first Bible lesson.

To let the sheer weight of the parable sink in deeper, he had me reread the very last sentence: "And throw that worthless servant outside, into the darkness, where there will be weeping and gnashing of teeth" (Matthew 25:30 NIV).

"Craig," he went on, "I was that third servant. I did not waste my talent on gambling, prostitution, or crime, but I also did not grow it. I felt guilty about how much money I was already making. So, I hid my talent."

Nine months earlier, even before I was a believer, Clarke had engaged our firm to improve his culture, team dynamics, and customer experience. He didn't want or need growth.

Eventually, I challenged him. "Let's grow this anyway to create more jobs in this amazing culture and allow more clients the opportunity to be served in this way. If you don't want more money, cap your personal income, and give the rest away."

He decided to triple his business and give two-thirds to his church and other ministries. Fast forward a number of years, and he added more than another zero to the growth and used his business primarily as a vehicle to witness to people and fund Kingdom works.

That was my entry into God's Word as a new believer. God blessed me with some amazing experiences, teachers, and wisdom that I didn't fully grasp or appreciate at the time. As I've walked with the Lord, He has given me ever deeper insights into the role of business leaders and doing business for the Kingdom.

According to the Bible, as believers we are "a royal priesthood" (1 Peter 2:9 NIV). He made us "a Kingdom and priests" (Revelation 1:6; 5:10). Even if you are a business leader not in traditional ministry, you are part of His Kingdom, and are one of His priests. Let that sink in. You are a priest!

As priests, the businesses we own or departments we lead are then "churches in the marketplace," and churches have two primary purposes: disciple believers to be more like Christ and witness to non-believers. Those should therefore be the purposes of our businesses.

Further, the marketplace is the biggest, most strategic mission field we have. One hundred percent of the lost are there—working, shopping, running errands, getting their vehicles serviced, and more. Most are not in church. The marketplace is the only place to reach them.

Plus, the marketplace is where all money is made. The government only prints money. Businesses make it. As business leaders, we have the ability to directly create more income, cash flow, and wealth. That gives us even more influence.

Therefore, business leaders have the ability to influence multitudes of people. This includes our families, employees, customers, suppliers, as well as the communities we do business in, the non-profits we support, and even the politicians whose campaigns we help fund.

The more successful our businesses are, the more influence we can have for the Kingdom. So, please embrace that. We need more Christian-owned businesses to grow and flourish and employ more and more people and serve more customers, just like Clarke decided to do.

A verse that stops many Christian business people from maximizing their business and influence is Matthew 6:24, which states, "You cannot serve both God and money" (NIV).

A good motive—that we do not want to serve money—can also miss the mark. We can inadvertently serve money by letting it stop us from growing. We can let fear get in the way, like that third servant.

Matthew 6:33 says, "But seek *first* the Kingdom of God and his righteousness, and all these things will be added to you" (ESV, emphasis mine). We should always ask God what He would have us do with our businesses and how to use our businesses to bring His Kingdom to earth.

We do so by embracing our calling as part of the royal priesthood and seeing our businesses as churches. But we have to be careful. As we embrace our priestly roles in the marketplace, we become ever more dangerous to the Enemy.

Satan will tempt us to focus on making money, so that we can give more to the church or a ministry, but that is different from seeking the Kingdom first. Our first priority should be seeking how we can influence ever more people for the Kingdom, trusting God will provide the resources, just as He promises.

Further, we also have to do business by the book. We should have "honest weights and scales."[13] We should "Give back to Caesar what is Caesar's and to God what is God's" (Mark 12:17 NIV). We should "not oppress a hired worker"[14] and "give him his wages"[15] and so much more.

We cannot do business the world's way. We cannot cheat on taxes, oppress workers, overcharge customers, and then think that our offering on Sunday will be accepted. "The Lord detests the sacrifice of the wicked, but the prayer of the upright pleases him" (Proverbs 15:8 NIV).

In conclusion, Luke 12:48b states, "From everyone who has been given much, much will be demanded; and from the one who has been entrusted with much, much more will be asked" (NIV).

As Christian business leaders, we have been given much (the ability to create income and wealth) and have been entrusted with much (the ability to influence multitudes of people)—in America, the most prosperous and powerful nation the world has known. The marketplace is the biggest mission field we have, and one in which all the lost can be found. Therefore, much will be demanded, and much more will be asked of us.

One day, just like in the parable of the talents, our Master will return. When He does, He will most definitely hold us accountable for what we did (the first two servants) or didn't do (the third servant) with what He entrusted us. Eternity hangs in the balance.

---

13 See Proverbs 11:1.
14 See Deuteronomy 24:14.
15 See Deuteronomy 24:15.

I, for one, want to hear the same thing the first two servants heard: "Well done, good and faithful servant!" (Matthew 25:23a NIV).

I hope and pray you do too—and will pursue that with me. Let's take our roles seriously and go all in together to redeem the marketplace for His Kingdom. "As iron sharpens iron, so one person sharpens another" (Proverbs 27:17 NIV).

Craig Hohnberger
Keynote Speaker, Business Coach
www.bujiactioncoach.com

CHAPTER 18

PERSONAL SPIRITUAL GROWTH: REFINING THE SOUL THROUGH BUSINESS CHALLENGES

Bob Willbanks

Embarking on a journey through the labyrinth of business, I've unearthed a pivotal truth: the essence of our character and faith is most vividly refined in the furnace of adversity. This narrative seeks to illuminate the transformative power of faith in the workplace, illustrating how the challenges we encounter can serve as conduits for profound spiritual growth and intimacy with God.

My odyssey into the depths of despair and back was marked by a series of choices that led me away from God, culminating in a night under the stark Minnesota sky where I blamed Him for my misfortunes. This period of my life was characterized by a relentless pursuit of success, marred by addiction and personal failure. Yet, it was in this nadir that God's grace intervened, embodied by my wife, Barb, and a newfound commitment to faith.

Re-engaging with Scripture was the first step on the path to redemption. This journey was not merely about habitual reading but about allowing God's Word to permeate my being, transforming my understanding of success, leadership, and service. It was here that I began to grasp the weight of Christ's yoke—a symbol not of burden, but of partnership and strength.

The Yoke of Christ: A Symbol of Intimate Relationship

Jesus invites us to take His yoke upon us, a call to enter into an intimate relationship with Him. This yoke, far from being a tool of restraint, is a symbol of unity and shared purpose. In my life, embracing this yoke meant reevaluating my definition of leadership. True leadership, I learned, is characterized by service, humility, and a steadfast reliance on God's direction.

Through this lens, the business challenges I faced became opportunities to demonstrate faith in action. I witnessed firsthand how leading with a Christ-centered approach not only brought peace and clarity to my endeavors but also influenced those around me. It became evident that our daily choices—whether to operate under the yoke of the world's expectations or Christ's gentle guidance—have profound implications on our personal and professional growth.

The Significance of Choices

Every day, we stand at a crossroads of decisions, each path marked by either the pursuit of worldly accolades or the humble walk with Christ. My journey from the brink of despair to a life of purpose underscores the power of choices grounded in faith. It's in the decision to let go of control and allow God to steer our lives that we find true freedom and success.

B.U.S.Y.: Being Under Satan's Yoke vs. Being Under Savior's Yoke

In the fast-paced rhythm of the business world, the term "busy" is often worn as a badge of honor. However, busyness can be a trap—Being Under Satan's Yoke—where the essential connections with God and those around us are neglected. The challenge lies in discerning between being busy for the Kingdom and being busy for the sake of busyness, which can lead to a life of unfruitful endeavors.

In our quest to navigate life through the lens of faith, the acronym B.U.S.Y. presents a compelling dichotomy between two states of busyness: Being Under Satan's Yoke versus Busy Under Savior's Yoke. This distinction offers profound insights into how our alignment—either with the world's demands or with God's will—shapes our experiences and effectiveness.

Being Under Satan's Yoke

Under Satan's Yoke, busyness becomes a distraction, leading us away from God's purpose for our lives. It is characterized by:

- Striving: A relentless pursuit of personal achievements at the expense of spiritual growth.
- Immediate and Urgent: A focus on the here and now, prioritizing temporary needs over external values.
- Self-Centered: Actions and decisions driven by personal gain rather than the welfare of others.
- My Truth: Embracing relative truths that align with personal desires, ignoring the absolute truth found in Scripture.
- Willful: Relying on one's strength and wisdom, neglecting the need for divine guidance.
- Restless: A constant state of unease, devoid of the peace that comes from trusting in God.
- Identity in Self: Finding worth in accomplishments, possessions, or social status, rather than in our identity as children of God.

Busy Under Savior's Yoke

Conversely, being Busy Under Savior's Yoke transforms our busyness into a purposeful pursuit of God's kingdom. It embodies:

- Abiding: Remaining in constant fellowship with Christ, drawing strength and direction from Him.
- Eternal Mindset: Focusing on the everlasting impact of our actions, guided by the hope of eternal life.
- Others-Centered: Serving and loving others as an expression of our love for God.
- Absolute Truth: Adhering to the unchanging truths of Scripture as the foundation for all aspects of life.

- Submit and Obey: Willingly placing our plans under God's authority and following His lead.
- Restful: Experiencing peace amidst the hustle, knowing that our efforts are aligned with God's will.
- Identity in Christ: Recognizing that our true value comes from being loved and redeemed by Jesus, not from worldly achievements.

Reflect on your current state of busyness. Are you burdened under Satan's yoke, or are you experiencing the freedom and fulfillment that comes from being yoked with our Savior? This examination is not meant to induce guilt but to invite a shift in perspective—from striving in our strength to abiding in Christ's. As we align our efforts with God's will, we find that our work not only bears fruit but also brings deep satisfaction and peace.

The Fruit of the Spirit: A Measure of Our Walk

Galatians 5:22–23 introduces us to the fruit of the Spirit, the true measure of our walk with God. In my life, the transition from a state of spiritual barrenness to one rich with love, joy, peace, patience, kindness, goodness, faithfulness, gentleness, and self-control was marked by a conscious choice to embrace the yoke of Christ. This fruit is not merely a personal benefit but a testament to God's presence in our lives, influencing our actions and interactions within the business sphere.

Encouragement for the Reader

You, too, can experience the transformative power of living under Christ's yoke. In the bustling arena of business, where pressures and temptations abound, let this principle guide your actions and decisions. Consider the impact of your choices, not just on your career, but on your spiritual journey and those you lead.

Matthew 11:28–30 offers a profound insight into the nature of Christ's yoke: "Come to me, all you who are weary and burdened, and

I will give you rest. Take my yoke upon you and learn from me, for I am gentle and humble in heart, and you will find rest for your souls. For my yoke is easy and my burden is light" (NASB). This passage underlines the promise of growth, peace, and rest that comes from walking in step with Jesus.

The Promise of the Yoke of Christ

As the yoke of Christ symbolizes an intimate partnership with Jesus, it promises not only to guide us but to multiply our effectiveness. As I leaned into this relationship, I discovered that my burdens were lightened, my purpose clarified, and my influence expanded beyond my capabilities. This yoke does not constrain us; rather, it frees us to achieve greater heights, powered by divine strength and wisdom.

Life Balance Wheel vs. Centered Life on God

The conventional concept of a life balance wheel encourages us to segment our lives into compartments, striving for equilibrium among them. Yet, this approach often leads to a fragmented existence, constantly chasing after elusive balance. In contrast, a life centered on God offers a singular focus that permeates and harmonizes all aspects of life. As we center our lives on Christ, we find that balance naturally flows from the inside out, guided by the Holy Spirit.

As you navigate the complexities of integrating faith with your professional endeavors, remember that the journey is not about achieving perfection but about continuous growth and reliance on God. Let the principles of choices, the dangers of busyness, the cultivation of the fruit of the Spirit, the embracing of Christ's yoke, and the centered life on God guide your path.

Matthew 11:28–30 remains a cornerstone of this journey, inviting us to experience the rest and empowerment that comes from yoking ourselves with Christ. This passage is a beacon for all who seek to navigate the business world without losing sight of their spiritual anchor.

The integration of faith into the marketplace is not merely a lofty ideal but a practical pathway to personal and professional fulfillment. By making choices aligned with God's will, understanding the true cost of busyness, bearing the fruit of the Spirit, accepting the yoke of Christ, and centering our lives on Him, we can transform not only our businesses but our very souls.

Bob Willbanks
CEO, G7 Networking
www.g7networking.com or www.ndp-tc.com

CHAPTER 19

UNIFIED IN MISSION: CRAFTING A COLLECTIVE CHRISTIAN BUSINESS VISION

Steve Ahearn

"Passive Income" is the buzz phrase on every wealth-building site and webcast lately—and for good reason. Creating cash flow when you sleep is a tremendous way to build net worth. Building a business that produces revenue without requiring one to be actively involved with every transaction removes the limitations of the traditional business model, trading time for money. By replacing individual effort with a system that generates and fulfills consumer interest, an entrepreneur can be in multiple places at the same time! Just as the launching of a rocket takes 90 percent of the energy for the entire mission, building a passive income stream requires a great deal of work up front, but done correctly, that work will pay dividends for years. The automation of the income stream allows the merchant to refine and grow the business instead of hustling to create daily revenue. The consumer is happy as they are provided better service and product enhancements because the owner can work *on*, not *in*, the business. This is the success spiral that consultants preach, and entrepreneurs strive to perfect.

While the above paragraph may be true, what does it have to do with the title of the chapter, "Unified in Mission: Crafting a Collective Christian Business Vision?" It's also true that every day, every merchant engages in passive evangelism. If this practice can become intentional, united, and consistent, the business community can lead a national revival that shows the world what it means to have Jesus in your heart every day—not just on Sunday. Every day of your business life decisions are made—some simple, some complex. Those decisions are observed by your customer base. With each decision, you are preaching your sermon. Is your message one of love, honesty, fairness, generosity? Or are you taking advantage of people, treating employees poorly, and cheating investors instead? The thing about passive evangelism is that you cannot turn it off. What you do is tangible proof of who you are. All the time. You are either leading people to the cross or you are a stumbling block.

> *"In the same way, let your light shine before others, so that they may see your good works and give glory to your Father who is in heaven."* (MATTHEW 5:16 ESV)

Imagine a world in which all Christian-owned businesses identified themselves to the public and operated along a united belief in the basic biblical principles of fairness, honesty, hard work, and integrity. By operating intentionally by God's design, these businesses would be successful, as God defined the success of that business. If a business is operating in the light, then the owners will be happy, busy, accomplished people—the exact kind of business to which customers would be attracted.

Imagine all of these magnets in a myriad of locations and industries—all attracting the public's attention. A consumer trading across a spectrum of businesses would notice that these Christian businesses are well-run, respectful, and honest. Not only would consumers seek them out for commerce, but they would also start seeking out Christian businesses for deeper answers. This collective of business owners, by living their faith in plain sight, becomes a powerful force in changing people's spiritual lives. One business owner doing this on their own will have some impact within their sphere of influence. The massive power of passive evangelism is in the breadth of the message.

Will this collective make a difference? Is there a need to organize the Christian business community? There are over 33 million small businesses in the USA, employing over 61 million people, processing millions of transactions per day. Mr. Google says that 63 percent of the U.S. is Christian.[16] Simple math, very simple, indicates that around 20 million small businesses and 40 million employees are Christian. That same math indicates that 13 million businesses and 21 million employees are *not* Christian. Common sense dictates that the power of 20 million businesses joining together to operate under a biblical charter would make a huge difference. Millions of transactions completed under divine guidance are millions of data points to the believer and millions of micro-witness opportunities for the non-believer. Is there a need? Definitely! There are 21 million non-Christian business people that need to change their eternity. If we don't show them God in our daily actions, who will? This job is too big for preachers and missionaries. We are all called to be the messenger for someone.

If we agree that passive evangelism from the business community is needed and can fundamentally change society, how do we do it? Saint Bernard of Clairvaux, who lived from 1090–1153, is supposed to have said this: "The pathway to hell is paved with good intentions."[17] To create a revolution, you need sound doctrine, uncorruptible leadership, and willing disciples. The good news is that we have two out of the three. The Bible is sound doctrine and Jesus is uncorruptible. We need disciples. The first step for the disciples would be to craft the charter. It would need to be biblically sound, not denominationally sound. Once we have the charter, it would have to be introduced to the business community. The business community would join the collective and identify themselves as members, so that the community would know what to expect. Businesses would need to communicate

---

16 Gregory A. Smith, "About Three-in-Ten U.S. Adults Are Now Religiously Unaffiliated," Pew Research Center's Religion & Public Life Project, December 14, 2021, https://www.pewresearch.org/religion/2021/12/14/about-three-in-ten-u-s-adults-are-now-religiously-unaffiliated/.
17 "The Road to Hell Is Paved with Good Intentions," Wikipedia, December 22, 2023, https://simple.wikipedia.org/wiki/The_road_to_hell_is_paved_with_good_intentions.

with one another to offer support and ensure accountability. This is a huge undertaking that many groups are trying to develop. The juice is worth the squeeze, as proved by the statistics above. According to Jesus, "What is impossible with man is possible with God" (Luke 18:27 ESV).

WIFM? (What's in it for me?) I am a business owner and have been most of my adult life. I understand that it is easy to write a chapter and talk about running a godly business in conjunction with other business owners around the country. I also understand the fear of announcing that you are a Christian business. Are you going to lose non-Christian customers? Are you going to offend someone? What happens if you mess up? All those same fears kept me from being a visible Christian business person for a long time. It has taken many years to realize that if I put God first, everything will work out okay. It is a lesson I am still learning. What I can share is this: if you make God your CEO and run all your decisions by Him, you will have success, peace of mind, and a fundamentally sound business—a business that will flourish.

In conclusion, there is a clear need for creating a collective with a shared biblical business vision. The results of such a collective would change lives, communities, and society at large. This is too important to wait for someone else. Find an organization, call fellow business owners in your own town, and make the individual decision to run your business in a way that is congruent to the Bible. Passive evangelism works! Make sure you are sharing the right message. Let your light shine so that others see God.

Steve Ahearn
Founder, Talents Rewards
www.talentsrewards.com

CHAPTER 20

THE FUTURE AWAITS: EMBRACING GOD'S VISION FOR KINGDOM ENTREPRENEURS

Joy Dawson

Would you agree that vision, if not the most important of our five senses, has little to do with *sight* at all? *Vision* is defined as the ability to imagine how a country, society, industry, and so on, will develop in the future, and further, to have the ability to plan for that in a suitable way. As Helen Keller once said, "The only thing worse than being blind is having sight but no vision."[18] In a world often clouded by uncertainty, having a clear vision is essential for the growth and sustainability of not only businesses, but also the Kingdom. Without vision, there is no execution, and nothing is accomplished. Proverbs 29:18 says, "Where there is no vision, the people perish: but he that keepeth the law, happy is he" (KJV). The NIV translates it like this: "Where there is no revelation, people cast off restraint; but blessed is the one who heeds wisdom's instruction." *Vision* is the view of the future.

In the quest to embrace God's vision for Kingdom entrepreneurs, we find ourselves on a journey filled with purpose, faith, and divine guidance. The future awaits, and as stewards of God's gifts, we are called to navigate this entrepreneurial path with intentionality and a profound connection to *His* vision. In the bustling world of entrepreneurship, where strategies are crafted and dreams are woven into business plans, there lies a profound calling for Kingdom entrepreneurs.

---

18 Helen Keller, "Helen Keller - the Only Thing Worse than Being Blind Is...," Brainy Quote, accessed February 5, 2024, https://www.brainyquote.com/quotes/helen_keller_383771.

As we dive into the visions the Creator has placed in His disciples, we will turn the sacred pages of Scripture, seeking guidance and inspiration for the path that lies ahead.

In the realm of Kingdom entrepreneurship, purpose becomes the compass guiding our business endeavors. As we weave our skills, passions, and divine calling together, our businesses become vessels through which God's vision unfolds. Proverbs 16:3 reminds us to "commit to the Lord whatever you do, and he will establish your plans" (NIV). Success is not solely measured in profit margins, but in alignment with God's purpose. It is a commitment to divine principles, a steadfast dedication to ethical business practices, and a recognition that our endeavors are woven into the fabric of God's plan.

That being said, life isn't always rainbows and unicorns; as a matter of fact, it is quite the opposite. The Enemy has come to kill, steal, and destroy, and as we lean into the Word of God and know our purpose, he tries to confuse that assignment relentlessly. If we anchor our hope in God though, He will guide us through the uncharted waters and storms of life. In any success story, there is always failure. Kingdom entrepreneurship is no different, but Psalm 37:4 gives us hope. It states, "Delight yourself in the Lord, and he will give you the desires of your heart" (ESV).

Embracing God's vision requires unwavering faith in the face of challenges and uncertainties. Kingdom entrepreneurs find strength by leaning on their faith, and understanding that their ventures are not solitary pursuits, but *partnerships with the Divine*. Through prayer, trust, and resilience, we overcome obstacles—knowing that God's plan is unfolding in our entrepreneurial journey. Embrace the vision He instills within you and witness His Kingdom as it unfolds through your unique contribution. God's Kingdom is a collective of visionaries, in which each purposeful dream aligns with His sovereign plan.

In the Kingdom entrepreneur's toolbox, prayer and seeking divine guidance are indispensable. God's vision is revealed through moments of reflection, meditation, and spiritual discernment. As we listen to His guidance, we gain insights that transcend conventional wisdom, shaping our decisions and strategies in alignment with His divine plan. The future of Kingdom entrepreneurship is marked by businesses that reflect the values of this Kingdom.

Standing on truth in all things—from ethical practices to fostering inclusivity and compassion—our ventures become beacons of light in the marketplace. By integrating Kingdom values into every aspect of our businesses, we contribute to a world where God's love and principles are made manifest in the economic sphere. The Kingdom entrepreneur understands the power of collaboration. In a world interconnected by technology and relationship, we leverage partnerships that amplify our impact. Together, we create a network of entrepreneurs committed to advancing God's vision for a transformative and purpose-driven marketplace.

As we embark on this journey into the future, let us do so with hearts open to God's guidance, minds attuned to *His vision*, and hands ready to build businesses that glorify the Kingdom. The future awaits! And it is not just a destination; it is an ongoing journey of discovery, innovation, divine alignment, and healing. God's Word urges, "Turn my eyes away from worthless things; preserve my life according to your word" (Psalm 119:37 NIV).

In and through this process, we find His joy, not only in our destination, but in the transformative process that shapes our businesses and ultimately, our souls. The future truly awaits, and in embracing God's vision for Kingdom entrepreneurs, we discover a path that leads not only to prosperity, but to a legacy of divine impact.

> *"Then the Lord replied: 'Write down the revelation and make it plain on tablets so that a herald may run with it. For the revela-*

tion awaits an appointed time; it speaks of the end and will not prove false. Though it linger, wait for it; it will certainly come and will not delay.'"

(Habakkuk 2:2–3 niv)

This passage emphasizes the idea of patiently waiting for God's vision to unfold in its appointed time, highlighting the certainty and fulfillment of His plan. In the Kingdom, we prepare for such a time as this! The future awaits, awakening His vision for the Kingdom!

Our vision as citizens of the heavenly Kingdom is not confined by earthly limitations. It's a glimpse into God's eternal design, urging us to live with heavenly perspective in every earthly endeavor! Without God, a vision is but a fleeting mirage, lacking the substance that gives it eternal significance and profound meaning. Ultimately, God's vision for our life is abundantly more than our minds can ever imagine. He wants us to become more like Him as He reveals Himself to us in Christ; and in being like Him, we will come to behold Him face to face in perfect communion.

God gives us a clear vision of His expected end: "'For I know the plans I have for you,' declares the Lord, 'plans to prosper you and not to harm you, plans to give you hope and a future'" (Jeremiah 29:11 niv). He has a plan for our life and living. Therefore, this vision (*His plan*) becomes the standard by which we judge every decision, so that we might reach God's desired destiny for our lives. This is the future (and the power) that Kingdom entrepreneurs hold—this is the power of *vision*. Where there is no vision, there is no hope. Vision with action can change the world. Kingdom entrepreneurs, God will illuminate your vision. The future awaits!

Joy Dawson
Founder of Joyfully Planned Firm
www.joyfullyplanned.com

CHAPTER 21

THE POWER OF IDENTITY: UNDERSTANDING WHO WE ARE IN CHRIST

Chet Gladkowski

Our identity is either in Christ or somewhere else. There's no middle ground. Period.

In today's world, songs like "I Gotta Be Me" and "My Way" declare the unshakable truth that we are the kings of our own identity. We choose who we are, forcing it on everyone else. This powerful identity belief rings true in some surprising places. When Queen Elsa tells herself to "Let It Go" in *Frozen*, she's telling the world that she's free to choose her identity.

Along with Elsa, our modern culture tells us to look *within* to find our inner identity. We're the only ones who get a vote. No one else gets to choose for us. Each person gets to determine their identity. However, there are severe problems inherent in choosing our own identity. Choosing it doesn't give us the power or stability to hold up under the pressures of modern daily living or persecution.

Is it any wonder that depression and suicide rates have climbed? "The percentage of U.S. adults who report having been diagnosed with depression at some point in their lifetime has reached 29%, nearly ten percentage points higher than in 2015.... Americans who currently have or are being treated for depression has also increased, to 17.8%, up about seven points over the same period. Both rates are the highest recorded by Gallup since it began measuring depression … in 2015."[19]

---

19 Dan Witters, "U.S. Depression Rates Reach New Highs," Gallup.com, September 14, 2023, https://news.gallup.com/poll/505745/depression-rates-reach-new-highs.aspx.

When adjusted for population growth and age, the suicide rate has also risen—to 37% since 1999![20]

There is no stability when *we choose* our identity. Think about it for a minute: How many times have we changed our mind about who we are? What do we want to do? Who do we want to be? There's no strength, stability, or steadiness in choosing our own identity.

However, when we become a Christian, our identity is placed in Jesus. When all our sins—past, present, and future—are covered in the one-time sacrifice of Jesus on the cross, our identity is forever changed and secure. Not by who we are or what we've done, but by who God is and what He's already done.

> *"Anyone who belongs to Christ has become a new person. The old life is gone; a new life has begun!"*
>
> (2 Corinthians 5:17 NLT)

Our identity in Christ is never earned. It's given to us by God's grace through faith.[21] This makes us humble because there's nothing we can do to earn it! We were such sinners that God Himself had to die for us![22]

At the same time, our identity is lifted up to the heavens because God accepts us. He loves us. He'll never turn away from us. We are His children. We can run to our great heavenly Father and boldly fly into His arms.

If you have an identity based in Jesus Christ, success might bother you a little bit. It might go to your head a little bit, but it will never completely throw you. Failures upset and discourage, but you know

---

20 Heather Saunders and Nirmita Panchal, "A Look at the Latest Suicide Data and Change over the Last Decade," KFF, August 21, 2023, https: //www.kff.org/mental-health/issue-brief/a-look-at-the-latest-suicide-data-and-change-over-the-last-decade.
21 See Ephesians 2:8–9.
22 See Romans 5:6–8.

that it's just a job. It's just money. It doesn't affect your being able to stand sinless and faultless before the throne of God.

When our identity is securely in—and through—Jesus, we're free. This is an identity that's radically different than any other. It's perhaps the most wonderful and unique part of the Christian gospel.

Only One Place

Our identity is either in Christ or somewhere else. There's no middle ground. Think of it this way. Imagine we are going to drive to Canada. Until we cross the border, we're in the United States. We can put our toes right up against that painted border line, but we're still in America. It's only after crossing the border that we're in Canada.

The same is true with our identity in Jesus. When we give our lives to Christ, we can never be separated from His love.[23] Our eternal identity and destiny are set—once and for all. We are, and always will be, under God's never-ending love. His extravagant, unconditional, continual love changes everything.

Our New Identity in the Marketplace

This new identity in Christ has significant and powerful ramifications. While it starts with our personal and intimate relationship with God, it doesn't stop there. Our new identity spills over into our workplace in three ways.

- **Our Careers:** We no longer get our identity through our work, income, status, or achievement. Instead of being driven by success or greed, we're willing to say with James: "If it is the Lord's will, we will live and do this or that" (James 4:15 NIV).
- **Our Relationships:** Since all people are made in the image of God,[24] and Jesus died for each one of us,[25] we'll treat all people as special. We'll put a premium on people, treating them with

---

23 See Romans 8:38–39.
24 See Genesis 1:27.
25 See 2 Corinthians 5:15.

respect and dignity.[26] We'll listen to (and serve) others—regardless of their place in society.

- **Our Goals:** If we really believe that "for me, to live is Christ and to die is gain" (Philippians 1:21 NIV), then our goals for this life become temporary. We'll place increased importance on becoming the godly person He wants us to become and invest in our relationships with both coworkers and even competitors.

A Living Example

A new employee of a major television network made a mistake—the kind of mistake that people get fired for. And they should have been, except for their manager. The manager stepped forward and took the blame. In front of the management team, the boss explained that the root cause of the mistake was improper and incomplete training. Since they were responsible for this, the fault lay with them. Now this manager has earned a reputation for high-quality work and being a great team player. While they took a hit on their reputation, both the manager and employee kept their jobs.

As you can imagine, the employee was greatly relieved, and repeatedly thanked their boss, but the manager just brushed it aside, saying they should just move on. But the employee couldn't let it go.

You see, in that place and in that industry, everyone took credit for someone else's work or placed the blame on others. No one ever helped anyone else. So, over and over, the employee asked why the manager had done this highly unusual thing. Why did they take the blame? What would make them do this?

Finally, the frustrated manager looked the employee in the eye, and saying they were going to only say this once, shared that they were Christian, and at that the center of their faith was God taking the

---

26 See 1 Peter 2:17.

blame for them on the cross. As a follower of Jesus, they were to do the same thing. And so, they had.

Stunned, the only words that came out of the employee's mouth were, "So, where do you go to church?" This example of Jesus at work made them want to check it out for themselves.

It's easy to want mountaintop experiences. But most of the living done here on planet Earth is backstage, where no one can see. Where one life touches another. Where one kind word soothes a wound and encourages the hurt.

May we take our new identity in Christ to the world. Starting right where we are. In our workplace. With our coworkers. Living for Jesus before a watching world.

Chet Gladkowski
Creator of National Day of Hope
www.nationaldayofhope.net

CHAPTER 22

BUILDING TO LAST: FOUNDATIONS IN JESUS FOR ENDURING SUCCESS

Ford Taylor

Everyone needs a thick and solid foundation—built to last and founded in Jesus—for enduring success. When I started reading the Bible through a different lens, things changed in my career. I began reading past the chapter numbers and through the breaks and commas, being sure to continue reading anytime I saw a connecting word: such as, like, if, therefore, and so many others. I recognized how much practical and implemental sense the Bible actually made.

One thing that really hit me was *the way* Jesus led. He gave everything He had. He followed His Father without reserve and focused on Him above all else. Paul later wrote: "Do not conform to the pattern of this world but be transformed by the renewing of your mind. Then you will be able to test and approve what God's will is—his good, pleasing, and perfect will" (Romans 12:2 NIV). While we talk a lot about the importance of the transformation of the mind found in this verse, we should also remember the one before it that says, "I urge you, brothers and sisters, in view of God's mercy, to offer your bodies as a living sacrifice, holy and pleasing to God—this is your true and proper worship" (Romans 12:1 NIV).

What does that mean? It means that *everything we do is worship*. If you think of your life and work—how you treat your employees, customers, and families, as well as how you drive and answer emails—as *worship*, it will definitely change your thinking. As you submit yourself to God, your life will overflow into others for good.

Later, Paul says that your purpose is to become more like God's Son, so that His Son would have lots of brothers and sisters. God's plan was to create a huge family devoted to loving Him and each other. If that's true, and you already lead through the V.S.T.T.E.E.L.E. model I mentioned in chapter three, what else could you do to accelerate the growth of your organization? One tool you can create is called V.P.M.O.S.A. and focuses on achieving your personal goals.

An anecdotal story illustrates it best: One day, Alfred Nobel picked up the newspaper and read that he had supposedly died when, in reality, it was his brother, Ludwig, who had passed away. As he read what the newspaper said about him, he realized he would forever be remembered primarily as the man who created dynamite. His name was forever linked to an invention that killed people. He decided he didn't want to be remembered that way. What did he do about it? He came up with the Nobel Peace Prize, so he would be remembered for peace rather than death and destruction.

Just as Alfred Nobel did, take time to consider your legacy. It could be one of the most important things you ever do. As you contemplate your dreams and identify your goals, here are a few things to consider. Take the time to answer these three questions:

1. What do you want your tombstone to say?
2. When you die, what do you want said about you at your funeral? How do you want your spouse, children, friends, and coworkers to remember you?
3. Based on your tombstone and obituary, what values should you be living out—here and now?

After you've written down some thoughts about these questions, let me help you embark on what we refer to as the **V.P.M.O.S.A.** *This process is one of the most powerful tools a transformational leader can adopt.* You can use it—not only for yourself on a personal level, but also with your organization. The same questions can apply to both.

Creating Your V.P.M.O.S.A.

V = Vision

What future reality are you pursuing? What do you dream of accomplishing? Where are you going as a leader? Write down your thoughts. This is your vision statement.

P = Purpose

Why would you pursue this vision? Why are you here on earth? This is your purpose statement.

M = Mission

What are you willing to do (that others may not be willing to do) to see your vision become a reality? What sets you apart? That is your mission statement. (Just a note. Please remember as you write out these three statements to not get bound up in the semantics of which one is which. Just think about and answer the reflective questions above to the best of your ability.)

O = Objectives

Next, identify three to five objectives that you want to accomplish in the next twelve to eighteen months that will move you toward your vision, purpose, and mission. These objectives are your goals as a leader. After you have experienced this part of the **V.P.M.O.S.A.** process for a while, it would be good for you to make it a habit of writing down five to six other objectives on an annual or a regular basis. I suggest that you break down your objectives into four quadrants:

1. Family
2. Work (income-producing activity)
3. Health (mental, emotional, physical, and spiritual)
4. Community (in which you give back with no expectation of anything in return)

When these four quadrants are in balance, I have a special place of peace and am more able to positively impact others. Balancing these areas *does not mean making them equal*. Different quadrants will take more or less of your time, based on your season of life. Let's use the example of coaching a child's sports team to illustrate. This activity would combine the areas of family, community, and, if you do some of the running or workouts with the team, physical health. In that case you would be doing three of the four quadrants at the same time. Learn to change your thinking from Work/Life balance to Life/Work balance. Now, on to the **S.A.!**

S = Strategies

Identify two to three strategies that will help you reach each objective you've named.

A = Actions

Now, identify specific actions you would need to take to implement each strategy within the next twelve to eighteen months. What specific, measurable actions would you take to execute these strategies? Again, don't get bound up in the semantics of whether something is an objective, strategy, or action step. Just write them down and go for it. Getting them on paper and identifying them is the most important thing.

Applying Your V.P.M.O.S.A.

This process will make it much easier for you to prioritize your life, causing your stress levels to decrease significantly. It will help you simplify your decision-making processes. When there is a request for your time and energy, you will simply ask yourself, *Will this help me to fulfill my vision? Would this type of activity line up with my vision, mission, and purpose? Would it impact what I want others to say about me at my funeral? Would it influence the words on my tombstone?*

One of the things that's most important to me is my family. So, based on my **V.P.M.O.S.A.**, I check with my wife first thing when I get a phone call asking me to travel to consult, teach, or train. What would this commitment do to her schedule? What would this do to *our* schedule? What would this do to my schedule? Do my children have any important activities in that time that I should not miss?

The Value of Your V.P.M.O.S.A.

My **V.P.M.O.S.A.** has become a very practical guide for all the big—and small—decisions I make. If I didn't live and lead like this, what I want as my epitaph and obituary would never come to pass.

As you prioritize your life and leadership in this way, people will notice the results you begin to achieve. You may hear comments from others about "how lucky" you are. However, a **V.P.M.O.S.A.** doesn't lead to luck. Luck is what we call the point where the pathway of preparation intersects with the pathway of opportunity. When we are prepared and opportunity appears, we see that these intersections are points of destiny. So, it's really not about luck. *It's about preparation meeting opportunity.* That's what moves us toward the destiny we desire. That's how this process prepares you for the opportunities that come your way.

People often tell me how much they wish they had implemented this sooner. I can relate to that. The first time I did it, I ended up on the floor weeping as I compared what I had written with what the reality of my life reflected. Your life may not be as messed up as mine was relationally, so you may not experience this, but if you shed some tears, get comfortable with that. Those tears can help with the healing process.

I'd encourage you to make getting this done a top priority. If you'll take the time to write down your **V.P.M.O.S.A.**, you'll be able to look forward expectantly toward your vision. You'll also be able to look back on your life and see that those points from your past may not have been good luck or bad luck. Most likely, they were points of destiny that were moving you toward the fulfillment of the vision you've written down. *Enjoy the process* of creating your own **V.P.M.O.S.A.** You'll see that this leadership tool is one of the most effective steps you can take in becoming a transformational leader. One more suggestion: make part of your **V.P.M.** or one of your **O**bjectives to *become more like Jesus.*

After you do your personal **V.P.M.O.S.A.**, you do one for your company. Instead of a tombstone, think of it as a plaque on the wall. If people saw a plaque on the wall about you, your team, and your company fifty years from now, what would you want that plaque to say, so that everyone that read it would say, "Oh yeah, and they are definitely just as it says—a great team."

Take the time to write what you would want different groups to say if they were going to stand up and talk about you. Include your employees, their families, customers, bankers, vendors, competitors, and the community around you.

Then agree on five to ten **V**alues for the team to live out daily.

Follow the process above and finish a **V.P.M.O.S.A.** for the company or organization.

Vision: What are we going to accomplish?

Purpose: Why do we exist?

Mission: What are we willing to do (that others may not be willing to do) to accomplish the vision?

Write three to six very clear objectives or goals to accomplish over the next twelve to eighteen months with clear strategies and action steps.

If you'll do a **V.P.M.O.S.A.** for your personal life and another for your organization, it will accelerate you to the vision that God has given you personally, in your family, at work, in your community, and in health. If you'll connect that to the definition, purpose, values, and attributes of a great leader (a transformational leader) shared in chapter three, you will find a life/work balance and a much more peaceful life in every sphere in which you live, work, and play.

The other tool that I use is the *Social Covenant*. If you would like to see how that applies, please text the words "Social Covenant" to 53123 and you will get free access to that tool.

Work hard, play hard, rest hard, sleep hard, and pray hard. Success and peace are just around the corner.

Ford Taylor

Author, Keynote Speaker, Founder of FSH Strategy Consultants and Transformational Leadership

www.transformlead.com

CHAPTER 23

BUILDING BRIDGES: CONNECTING COMMERCE WITH YOUR BUSINESS STORY

David Welday

Recently I was leading a class on Sunday morning for kids in first through fifth grades. The topic was "Being Responsible." As is often the case, the lesson I was provided felt a little off track and in need of some improvement. So, I took some time to rewrite it. As I was thinking out how I could teach the kids what it meant to be responsible in a way that didn't just help shape their character but would pour into them spiritually, my mind was immediately drawn to two parables that Jesus taught, found in Matthew 25.

The first is the parable of the ten virgins—five of them were prepared and brought extra oil in case the bridegroom was delayed, and five did not. The next parable was about the master who entrusted his wealth to his servants—two of them invested wisely and one did not. Both of these parables gave me great material to use in helping my kids embrace the concept of being responsible.

Why share this story? Because Jesus was known for being a great teacher, and He used stories (parables) to help Him present His message well. Today, wise leaders in business also need to be effective communicators. To be an effective communicator, you must also be a good storyteller.

People don't often remember facts and statistics, but they do remember stories.

Why is that? Part of the reason is that stories touch us emotionally, whereas facts and statistics don't. Ask any sales professional about how to be more effective and they will quickly bring you to this critical point: emotion sells. It's not just sales rhetoric; it's science.

In the 1960s, two scientists, Roger W. Sperry and Michael Gazzaniga, conducted experiments revealing that the two halves of our brain are quite different. The left hemisphere is often associated with logic and analytical thinking whereas the right hemisphere is where our imagination, creativity, and intuition reside. Further study revealed that the side of our brain where most of us make decisions is the right side. Thus, leading to the philosophy that "emotion sells."

So, if you are leading a team and want to move them in a particular direction—if you want to be more persuasive in presenting your arguments or your position on a matter—find ways to *make your point with a story*.

Think about a memorable sermon you heard recently. Chances are there was a story told in that sermon that helped illustrate a key point of the message.

I was attending a seminar awhile back about communicating effectively through video. The presenter showed two promotional videos, both from chiropractic offices selling the services they provide the local community. The first video had the physician in a white lab coat, walking you through their offices and pointing out their state-of-the-art facilities, explaining how their "friendly and highly trained staff" were there to help you, as the patient, experience full recovery from whatever medical condition you faced that would require their services.

The second video took a very different approach. It opened with a scene from what appeared to be a local high school football game. Someone obviously took the video up in the bleachers. On the field, a player was on the ground, coaches and staff crowding around him. A narrator came on, saying, "Fifteen years ago, that young player on the field was me. It was my senior year. I was heading off to college soon and planned to go to med school to become a plastic surgeon. But in that moment, as I lay on my back, staring up at the faces leaning over me, I saw fear in their eyes. That's when I realized something: I could not feel my legs. I remember thinking: 'My life is over.' But over the next several weeks, doctors and physical therapists worked with me. Eventually I got the feeling back in my legs and was able to build up the strength to walk again. I decided right then and there that I wanted to dedicate my life to helping others regain mobility and get their lives back. I wanted to help others as my doctors had helped me."

What was the difference between the two videos? The first was professional and appropriately focused on the features and benefits that chiropractic office could offer. But the second video went in a different direction altogether. It told a story—and that story appealed powerfully to the emotions of the viewers. Which promotional video do you think was more effective?

This is just a simple example, but it illustrates my point: smart leaders are effective in leveraging the power of story to communicate and win the attention and loyalty of their audience.

So how about you? How can you use the power of story to connect with your audience more effectively? Here are some suggestions:

1. **Employ the power of testimonials.** Of course, you think the product or service you offer is great, but when *other people* say that what you offer is great, it carries greater weight with people who are most likely already predisposed to being skeptical and doubtful about your claims. While many of your testimonials should be very short, having just one or two sentences, a few should be a little longer. They should tell a story—a success story of how your product or service changed their life or made it better.

2. **Be willing to tell your own story!** What made you get into your business? Sometimes your own story can be a powerful

way to help people feel like they know you. Let's be honest, people want to do business with individuals and organizations they can trust. We are relational creatures, so choosing to be vulnerable enough to share a piece of your own story is a way to create connection and build trust with your audience.

Maybe you are in a highly competitive field, and there is truthfully not much difference between what you offer and what your competition offers. Sharing your story, the *why* behind the *what* that you do, may be just the thing that distinguishes you and sets you apart from the competition. Your story will resonate with your hearer.

3. **Help your customers see themselves in your story.** People are essentially selfish. We want to know what's in it for us. So, a good story needs to be one that not only grabs, and holds, people's attention, but one that engages them because they identify with it. In short, they must be able to picture themselves in the circumstance your story describes. When people can see themselves in your story, you have created a powerful connection that will hopefully lead to a sale.

What are some practical things you can do to inject the power of story into your marketing model?

Invite people to share their experiences with your product or service. Make it easy for people to do this. You might have a contest or a drawing where everyone who submits a testimonial gets their name entered into that contest.

Regularly "show and tell" the stories and testimonials you receive in video, text, and audio formats. Leverage your social media, email marketing, and website to do this. Change your stories regularly.

When highlighting the specific benefits that your product or service offers, make sure that each point you make is supported with a story. Use the feedback from personal customer experiences.

You are striving to run your business by Kingdom principles. The Bible is a storybook filled with the triumphs and struggles of fallible men and women that God nevertheless used to accomplish His purposes—to see His Kingdom come and His will be done on earth as it is in heaven. Make it your mission to boldly, consistently, and creatively tell your story and the story of your business as a way to connect with more people—and watch your business grow as a result!

David Welday
President, HigherLife Publishing and Marketing
www.higherlifepublishing.com

CHAPTER 24

SHINING LIGHTS: ROLE MODELS IN CHRISTIAN BUSINESS LEADERSHIP

Nate Chrisman

"Don't *try* to be a good role model."

These are the words I told my oldest son when I was tempted to tell him just the opposite. His four siblings hang on to every word he says and watch every move he makes. Often, they quickly replicate his behavior simply because of the influence he has as their older brother. At this moment, I did not want them to repeat his behavior, and I wanted to say, "Please be a good role model for your siblings."

For most, we can recall the names of the few or many individuals who have helped shape our lives. For some, the character you saw on display through their lives during a memorable experience of success, achievement, or even tragedy. Whether we observed them up close or from a distance, it was enough to make us say, "I want to be like them." For others, it was how an individual consistently showed up in our lives over and over again, making us better or calling us toward something more.

As I reflect on my life and my experience of being raised in a local Christian church congregation, Sunday mornings, Sunday nights, Wednesday nights, and usually a few more just for good measure, I have been taught countless times that I need to be a good example for those close to me who are watching and for the world who won't know any better how to live their lives if I do not become an example worth following. Then, as I gained more influence and affluence through business and leadership later in life, the famous words given to Peter Parker, a.k.a. Spider-Man, by his Uncle Ben, "With great power comes great responsibility," offer a cocktail of unbearable pressure to perform really well for all others. This is all in the name of being a good role model.

Can you see that somehow being a role model has been placed at the top of the list when it comes to living life as a Christian? This is only magnified as a Christian in business. Along the way, we made the tragic error that began in the garden. We have traded walking with God for *trying* to be like God. Eve was convinced by the enemy that her purpose was to become like God (Genesis 3:5).

The individuals we encounter in life that we would like to follow or become like are likely marked with some common attributes. These men and women in our lives exemplify positive character, integrity, and an unwavering commitment to what they believe. They put others before themselves, showing up for others with honesty and goodwill and meeting the needs of others. And, somehow, they are not easily shaken and remain grateful, positive, and optimistic in the face of difficult things.

Writers of New Testament Scriptures, Paul (1 Corinthians 13; Galatians 5), Peter (2 Peter 1), and even the recorded words of Jesus Himself spoke about these attributes (Matthew 7; John 15). They called them fruit. For much of my life, I've carried the weight of the idea that I must produce these attributes if I expect to please the Lord and impact others. **Keyword: I.** If I try hard enough to produce patience, eventually, I'll be patient. If I understand the nature of contentment and simply lay down my ambitions, desires, dreams, and passions, I will have the contentment thing figured out.

Here is the bottom line. Trying to "look the part" distracts you and me from actually living the part. Basically, we are saying, "I'm not a good example, but I'm going to try to be one. I'm not really as good as

I would like you to think that I am. So, I'll try really hard to be a good role model and example."Trying to be a good role model is simply fake and inauthentic and leads to shallow faith that looks like one thing on the outside but is something entirely different on the inside.

When I try to accomplish the "end goal" of producing good things on the outside, I lay down the goal of daily surrender and the work of God on the inside. This draws a line between living "for" God and living "with" God. Walking with God leads to living **present**—allowing me to show up as me, wherever I am, with enough faith for today, with **vulnerability**—allowing me to live authentically, with honesty about dreams, desires, struggles, and strengths, and with **purpose**—knowing that my only real goal is walking with the Lord today.

I could have used my words on these pages, finding heroes in faith and business to highlight and hold up as role models for us to follow. However, that may have only left us with more lists of things to do to become like those men or women we all admire so much. Instead, I chose to use my words to remind you, and myself, that being is better than doing. The men and women of faith who inspired us with their lives probably did not become that inspiration because they tried to become something they were not. Jesus said to His followers, "You *are* the light of the world...." His instruction was not to try and strive to become the light of the world.

I have learned that for better or worse, the inside you that no one can see will eventually lead to the outside you that everyone can see. Our faithfulness to walk daily with the Lord over time will produce *in* us the hope that others need. It will produce strength in weakness during difficult times. **It will produce good fruit without even trying**.

I told my son I did not want him to *try* to be a good role model. I refuse to put being a good example at the top of an arbitrary standards list of things my son must do. Rather, I want my son to be so connected to Jesus that the fruit of his life comes out really good. And, when the fruit is good, people might say, "He's such a good role model; you taught him well."

Nate Chrisman
Founder and CEO of I Want Good
www.iwantgood.org

CHAPTER 25

GROWTH AND GRACE: TRUSTING GOD TO DETERMINE YOUR STEPS

Eric Floyd

When I stop and reflect on the totality of my existence, it is glaringly evident that the grace of God has preserved me all the days of my life. Even throughout that prolonged season when I was by no means seeking His face, my Abba Father did not withdraw the hedge of protection that shielded yours truly from countless lethal threats—seen and unseen.

Similarly, the fact that a person with no theatrical training could somehow carve out a twenty-eight-year career as an entertainer at Universal Studios Orlando only further testifies how the Lord has unsparingly lavished his favor upon me.

In November of 2019, I was preparing a salad in my kitchen when my spirit heard God whisper, "Start a Christian podcast." At that time, I knew absolutely nothing about podcasting, the art of interviewing, recording equipment, or distribution, but after locking arms with some blind faith, I went for it. This decision would change the entire trajectory of my walk with Jesus—though not in the way one would expect.

The name I would give my podcast was of vital importance to me. I wanted it to embody everything I was as a Christian. One day while I was praying, the Holy Spirit advocated the title, *Where Grace Abounds*. This immediately resonated with me because when I share the details of my faith journey, one of the first things I always mention is, "It was the grace of God that set me free!"

In fact, my favorite verse in the entire Bible reads, "For God was in Christ, reconciling the world to himself, *no longer counting people's sins against them.* And he gave us this wonderful message of reconciliation" (2 Corinthians 5:19 NLT, emphasis mine).

Grace has the power to transform your life. Always remember, the Lord doesn't want to see his children barely survive. Instead, he wants them to utterly reign! The Word of God confirms this: "For if by one man's offence [Adam's] death reigned by one; much more they which receive *abundance of grace and of the gift of righteousness* shall reign in life by one, Jesus Christ" (Romans 5:17 KJV, emphasis and addition mine).

So, the Bible clearly spells out two criteria that must be met for you to "reign" in life—and neither of them can be "earned." First, if you want to reign in life, you must receive the "gift of righteousness." A supernatural transaction took place when Jesus died on the cross. He took our sin and replaced it with His righteousness. Evidence of this is also found in the Bible, which reads, "For our sake he made him to be sin who knew no sin, so that in him we might become the righteousness of God" (2 Corinthians 5:21 ESV). This means that if you have accepted Jesus Christ as your Lord and Savior, you are "the righteousness of God" in Christ. Period.

Secondly, if a Christian's desire is to reign in life, Romans 5:17 assures us that we receive an "abundance of grace" to accomplish this! What this *doesn't* mean is that a believer adopts this kind of mindset: "All right, Jesus, You saved me from hell, but I've got it from here!" So, let me encourage you—even when things are going great—pray daily for even more of God's unmerited and undeserved favor to rain down on your life. If you do, God's perfect Word promises that you will reign in every area where you choose to put your hand!

By His grace, God has guided my podcast down a divine thoroughfare, connecting me to places I never expected to go. I'll forever be thankful for a divine appointment I had toward the end of 2020. While searching the Internet for possible guests, I ran across a profile for "Krystal Parker—President, Central Florida Christian Chamber of Commerce." In hindsight, I'm sure the Holy Spirit must have sprinkled an extra spoonful of favor on the cold email invitation that I wrote to Krystal. The episode we recorded is one of my favorites to this day, but what I didn't realize at the time was how God was determining my steps when Krystal counseled, "You should think about joining the Christian Chamber yourself, Eric."

After hemming and hawing for a few months, I took Krystal's advice, and consequently became connected to the most sublime body of believers one can imagine. Unlike a normal chamber where most everything is "transactional," the Central Florida Christian Chamber of Commerce places priority on cultivating relationships and serving one another. It is truly "souls over sales"! I will be eternally grateful, not just for those authentic bonds I've made which will last a lifetime, but also for the way the Lord graciously allows me to regularly facilitate chamber gatherings where the presence and power of His Spirit is undeniable.

Although it really didn't come as a surprise when God asked Krystal to pass the Central Florida Christian Chamber of Commerce's presidential torch, so she could preside over the U.S. Christian Chamber of Commerce, it was definitely a surprise when she called and said, "We are officially launching the U.S. Christian Chamber of Commerce at the 2023 National Religious Broadcasters (NRB) Convention. God has put you on my heart to work our booth with us." For those unfamiliar with the NRB Convention, it is the largest gathering of Christian communicators on earth, and believe me when I say that during that four-day period, I experienced more than a few head-on collisions with the Holy Spirit.

I want to conclude with this thought: when God calls us to do something, things aren't always what they seem. Sure, I would love to have a world-renowned Christian podcast with millions of subscribers, and maybe someday I will. However, I find it nothing short of miraculous that *Where Grace Abounds* has supernaturally opened a door for me to continually partner with both the Central Florida Christian Chamber of Commerce *and* the U.S. Christian Chamber of Commerce concerning truly colossal Kingdom undertakings with effects that will echo throughout eternity. All this, just because I said yes to God one day while dicing up romaine lettuce in my kitchen!

Tune in and subscribe to *Where Grace Abounds* wherever you listen to your favorite podcasts!

Eric Floyd
Entertainer, Author, Podcast Producer
Eric.floyd@uschristianchamber.com

CHAPTER 26
FAITHFUL STEWARDSHIP: MANAGING RESOURCES GOD'S WAY
Shelsea Becker

In the intricate tapestry of the Christian life, the concept of biblical stewardship stands as a fundamental thread, guiding individuals toward a deeper understanding of managing their resources in accordance with God's principles. It goes beyond the realm of mere financial management; it encompasses the complete management of every facet of life, acknowledging the Creator's ownership of every possession and talent He has entrusted to us. The essence of stewardship finds its roots in the foundational truths found in the Bible:

"The earth is the Lord's, and everything in it."
(PSALM 24:1 NIV)

"To the Lord your God belong the heavens, even the highest heavens, the earth and everything in it."
(DEUTERONOMY 10:14 NIV)

"The heavens are yours, and yours also the earth; you founded the world and all that is in it."
(PSALM 89:11 NIV)

This realization—the understanding that our possessions, relationships, time, and abilities are not ours to possess, but ours to manage on behalf of our heavenly Father—forms the cornerstone of faithful stewardship. Furthermore, it reshapes our identity, redirecting our focus from our possessions to the One who rightfully possesses us. It's an outlook grounded in the acknowledgment that He is the Creator and Sustainer of all things.

> *"For in him all things were created: things in heaven and on earth, visible and invisible, whether thrones or powers or rulers or authorities; all things have been created through him and for him. He is before all things, and in him all things hold together."*
>
> (Colossians 1:16–17 NIV)

Godly stewardship fosters a redefined concept of success—measured not by worldly standards, but by the harmony between our actions and God's divine purposes, as well as the cultivation of godly character.

Author and top authority on personal finances, Ron Blue, defines *stewardship* like this: "Stewardship is the use of God-given resources for the accomplishments of God-given goals."[27] To embrace stewardship with a spirit of excellence, the initial step is nurturing and aligning your heart with God's. God loves you completely, and comprehending this fact fundamentally alters the manner in which we oversee His possessions. When we grasp that God's love serves as the power behind His Kingdom principles, we become more inclined to relinquish our personal agendas, cravings, and aspirations. In turn, His trust in us extends as an invitation to reciprocate that love by demonstrating care for Him and His people through the responsible utilization of His abundant resources.

This invitation to stewardship is beautifully illustrated in Matthew 25:23 in the parable of the talents, where the Master beckons us to "enter into the joy of your master." It's an invitation to join the Lord in stewarding all that He entrusts to us—promising us immense joy in the process. Managing resources according to God's principles is not only thrilling, but also yields benefits beyond our wildest imaginations. As we embrace this journey, we find our strength in the joy of the Lord. Understanding what brings delight to the Lord ultimately fortifies our faith. Embracing risk is an act of anticipation, as we observe

---

[27] Ron Blue, "What Is a Christian Financial Advisor?" Blue Trust, November 23, 2023, https://www.bluetrust.com/christian-financial-advisors/.

God's work unfolding before us. Adversity no longer intimidates us; instead, it energizes. It's good to remember that this parable emphasizes that being faithful in managing even the *smallest* portions leads to greater responsibilities. This highlights the inexhaustible generosity of the Giver who abundantly blesses us beyond our expectations.

James Lawless, a CEO as well as an author and speaker, said, "Christian stewardship is more than the management of things; it is the refusal to let things manage us."[28]

In order for my identity to be solely in Christ and not in anything I could obtain, the Lord used a relatively small thing to let me see the Big Picture. When I was a young mother with limited extra funds, I became infatuated with a pair of Jimmy Crystal sunglasses. They had sleek black rims adorned with Swarovski crystals—absolutely stunning. I was determined to have them! So, I scrimped and saved every dollar, quarter, and nickel until I could walk proudly out of that high-end boutique, feeling like a million dollars.

Sporting those remarkable glasses, weeks later I stepped into a restaurant and caught the attention of a college-aged lady who shared my enthusiasm for these shades. We instantly connected over their "fabulousness." During our meal, she approached our table again, admiring the glasses, now perched on my head. That's when a nudging stirred in my soul. I sensed the Lord urging me to give her my beloved Jimmy Crystal sunglasses. Can you imagine? I spent the rest of the meal debating with God, trying to explain my attachment to them and how much I'd sacrificed to own them. It was quite an internal struggle!

As we prepared to leave, our eyes met once more. Deep down, I knew that to obey God, I had to give her the sunglasses. Balancing my child on my hip, I leaned towards her, and asked if she would take the glasses off my head. She obliged, and I conveyed that they were now

---

[28] James Lawless, "Biblical Principles of Stewardship," Christ Church, accessed January 27, 2024, https://christchurch.us/stewardshipprinciples#: ~: text=-James%20Lawless%20.

hers. I had done it. I had obeyed. Yet, I departed the restaurant feeling far from content. I couldn't fathom why God would ask me to do that. I was bewildered and hurt.

A couple of weeks later, riding in my father's truck, I poured out my confusion to him. Despite obeying God, I still felt troubled. As I spoke, I rummaged through my purse and stumbled upon the velvet pouch for my sunglasses. Finding that felt like salt on a fresh wound. Once again, I was angry. However, in His gentle way, God nudged me to turn over the velvet pouch. There, in Swarovski crystals, were the letters "J" and "C"! J for Jesus and C for Christ—belonging to JC! It hit me like a lightning bolt. God was teaching me that everything belongs to Him, and we are mere stewards. In His grace, He was guiding me not to cling to worldly possessions because He is the ultimate Owner of everything. He was teaching me godly stewardship.

At the heart of this paradigm lies an understanding of God's economy—a divine economy that defies conventional logic. It's a truth echoed in the sacred text and observed in everyday life: "The last will be first, and the first will be last" (Matthew 20:16 NIV). It's an economy that extols humility and elevates the spirit of excellence, affirming that our identity as stewards does not merely reside in our possessions, but in our character.

Martin Luther, the fifteenth-century theologian, said, "I have held many things in my hands, and I have lost them all. But whatever I have placed in God's hands, that I still possess."[29]

The path of faithful stewardship is an ongoing journey, a constant surrender of our desires, ambitions, and possessions at the altar of divine ownership. It necessitates a reevaluation of our mindset, embracing the truth that we are not owners, but overseers, of all that

---

29 Martin Luther, "Luther-I Have Held Many Things in My Hands, and I... - Brainyquote," Brainy Quote, accessed January 28, 2024, https: //www.brainyquote.com/quotes/martin_luther_390009.

is entrusted to us. It invites us to emulate Christ, whose identity was rooted in His divine purpose—not in earthly possessions.

Therefore, let us embark on this journey of stewardship—entrusting all that we have and all that we are into the hands of the ultimate Owner, that we may indeed be faithful stewards in managing resources God's way.

Shelsea Becker
Founder and President of LYN Ministries
www.lynministries.org

CHAPTER 27
RESILIENCE AND RESTORATION: OVERCOMING SETBACKS WITH FAITH
The Path of Eileen Vazquez

In the heart of Orlando, Florida, a city where dreams flourish beneath the radiant sunshine, Eileen Vazquez has forged a path as a seasoned business owner and the driving force behind MS Consulting Firm, LLC. With over two decades of experience in the dynamic realm of human resources, Eileen's journey is a testament to resilience, determination, and an unwavering commitment to overcoming life's challenges.

Eileen's story begins in Puerto Rico, where she was born into a family seeking a better life in the United States. Her father, armed with only $1,000, no knowledge of English, and married to Eileen's hearing-impaired, English-speaking mother, embodied relentless pursuit and excellence. Their unwavering determination became the guiding light for Eileen, instilling in her a genuine desire to transcend the circumstances initially offered.

Her challenges persisted as Eileen was the only minority student in her school during the 70s and 80s. Motivated by her mother's unfulfilled dreams, Eileen embarked on her educational journey, choosing a community college while navigating the demanding terrain of a full-time job.

At the tender age of nine, Eileen faced a life-altering diagnosis of Type-1 diabetes that plunged her into a week-long coma. Emerging from this experience, she reacclimated into school life, where she often faced bullying for being different. This early encounter with adversity sowed the seeds of a deeper spiritual connection, leading Eileen to embark on a unique form of fasting—abstaining from secular music to honor her journey with God. All this at the age of nine!

As Eileen matured, the spirit within her grew bolder. Despite societal pressures, she felt a calling to speak the truth—to roar like a lion. This internal struggle accompanied her throughout college, corporate employment, marriage, and eventually single parenthood. Eileen faced struggles with what the "world" taught her was right; however, the spirit within her pulled at her and showed her a different way from the others. Eileen could not understand why she was battling so many things in life, *but the Lord had a reason for the trials.*

Undeterred by the demanding nature of her corporate career, Eileen pursued a self-directed education, earning a bachelor's degree in business administration and a master's degree in human resource management from the University of Phoenix. Her professional journey took root in the early days of the cell phone industry. Still, a career transition led her to discover her true passion in human resources (HR) at several Fortune 500 companies and in global healthcare.

The collapse of the housing market in 2008 and several corporate layoffs marked a turning point in Eileen's life, leading to her unemployment. With a newborn baby to care for, she had no choice but to apply for government assistance to provide food and milk for her child. This difficult situation became her teacher, giving her valuable lessons in strategy and resilience.

Starting over was not easy for Eileen, especially as she was in the midst of a divorce with a small child and minimal support from others. She felt isolated and cried out to the Lord, asking Him to make sense of it all. At her lowest point, she finally heard His voice. Intrigued, she started responding to altar calls, attending prayer meetings, and surrounded herself with His Word and His presence. In her prayers, she asked for discernment and wisdom, not knowing that this was just the beginning of what the Lord had planned for her. This spiritual journey was not without its challenges, as nightly demonic attacks sought to derail her path of obedience. Yet, Eileen clung to the mantra, "You become who you run to," reinforcing her faith with Scriptures on her office whiteboard: Amos 9:13–15, Psalm 91:1–16, and Matthew 5:3–16 all made their way up there. In addition, listening to a weekly prayer time with a well-known pastor helped her get up and move. She learned that the pain was not her problem, but the healing was her responsibility.

The cycle of fasting, consecration, rejection, refinement, and spiritual attacks were all part of her journey toward spiritual growth. She faced nightly attacks and finally realized the Enemy was trying to silence her because she carried the Lord within her. After looking back on her life, Eileen realized she had now faced spiritual warfare and understood that her purpose was to serve God's Kingdom people with her gift. What gift, you say? The gift of *human resources for His Kingdom.*

During this restoration time, God moved in a way that could only be seen by those who sought Him. Since 2020, He laid out a path for Eileen, a challenging one to follow because it was completely unknown. Little by little, it became clear that Eileen's purpose and life's work had been built *for such a time as this.* Eileen began serving as a small group leader at her local church, offering résumé assistance to those in need. (Two years later, the group continues to meet weekly and has up to twenty members!) The Holy Spirit continued to move by revealing the needs of small business owners with HR challenges who were unable to afford a full-time HR resource. Eileen made a Spirit-led decision to embark on an entrepreneurial journey, founding MS Consulting Firm, LLC—HR for Small Businesses. Today, the firm is an emerging HR consultancy, providing tailored solutions to small businesses in underserved communities in need. With over twenty years of experience, this firm has the skills to support employee relations, temporary and permanent staffing needs, risk management and compliance, and bookkeeping, and can also be the dedicated manager for each business owner.

Eileen's story is not merely a tale of personal triumph; it's a testament to the power of resilience, determination, and the pursuit of passion. Under her leadership, MS Consulting Firm is not just a business; it's a beacon of hope for small enterprises seeking reliable, efficient, and compliant HR solutions in the dynamic landscape nationwide.

The transformative business practices employed by Eileen Vazquez and MS Consulting Firm illuminate a new paradigm for success—one built on a foundation of faith, resilience, and a commitment to serving others. As businesses continue to navigate the challenges of the modern world, Eileen's journey stands as an inspiring example of how an unwavering spirit and a dedication to transformative business practices can lead to personal success and the creation of a positive impact on the community and beyond.

Where will the Holy Spirit lead next?

Eileen Vazquez
Founder, MS Consulting
www.msconsultingfirm.com

CHAPTER 28
GOD'S VIEW OF ECONOMY VS WORLDVIEW: PURPOSEFUL PROFIT AND DIVINE DISTRIBUTION

Kristi Nowrouzi

What does God care most about? The Kingdom of God. But what does that *mean*? I heard it defined as this: *Prioritizing spiritual well-being and our relationship with God above our worldly concerns.* Focusing on God's will and Word helps us to trust Him; lean on Him.

If I could be real with you right now, I spent most of my working life chasing after what *I* wanted. And it was usually to "look good." I wanted people to think I was successful, that I had made it. That usually shows up as name-brand things and lots of toys to enjoy. I guess what it boils down to is that I wanted to look important. What I didn't know then is that no one is looking at me in my car at the traffic light and thinking, "Wow, she must be successful and rich." No one! Those things aren't important, and we sure can't take them with us. I am so grateful that I have learned some lessons (the hard way, of course!) and grown in my relationship with and understanding of God.

I have been in the real estate and finance industries for twenty-three years. In that span of time, I have met thousands of people and worked with so many people that are really focused on appearing a certain way. I have analyzed thousands of credit reports and it's scary to see how much debt millions of people are walking around with. I believe it's because it's really easy to get pulled into the "gotta have it now" way of living.

This world has programmed our belief that "you deserve it," whatever that new and shiny "it" is. From cars to vacation packages to a pair of shoes or a purse that costs thousands of dollars, if we want it, there's a way to have it ... now. Instant gratification is the preferred taste when satisfying wants. Car payments that are a third of someone's take-home pay, multiple maxed-out credit cards, student loans and even personal loans that help pay for those things we can't seem to wait and save for. And that was me. Stretched to the max with debt. Some months I wasn't sure how I was going to pay the minimum payments and put gas in my expensive car. But I had to show up a certain way for the world. Or at least I thought so at the time.

As I have grown in my relationship with the Lord and enjoy a deeper understanding of the word, it has really helped reshape my perspective on striving at work and the choices I make with our finances. All of the answers are in the Bible!

Proverbs 1:7 says, "The fear of the Lord is the beginning of knowledge, but fools despise wisdom and instruction" (niv).

The Book of Proverbs has become my go-to reading material to remind me to plan. It's such a cliché, but when we fail to plan, we plan to fail. I would feel confident saying that the majority of people don't follow a budget, a plan. Could you imagine running a business without knowing what was coming in and what was going out in terms of money? We have to plan and then, more importantly, follow the plan! And we must also consider where our focus is. Have we gotten caught up with what the world says? I sure did. In nearly every way. I am so grateful for grace and guidance.

Let's look at how the world views money and finances and what the Bible says about money and finances.

The World	Striving	Certainty	Significance
The Word	Acceptance/ Gratitude	Love	Contributing/ Giving

The world really focuses on striving. I work in an industry where it is common to work seven days a week, regularly. I have been on the computer working at nine p.m. after starting my workday fourteen hours earlier. Can you relate? Many business owners, business leaders, the self-employed, and salespeople are all too familiar with this way of life. But at what cost? Precious time with our family and friends. Time to rest and reflect. Time to dream and plan. But the world seems to honor striving.

Your Net Worth Does NOT Equal Your Self Worth

The world chases after certainty. You may know people who stay in a job they hate because of health insurance or a guaranteed paycheck. Or perhaps stay in a relationship because the other person is loyal (not because they are in love). Certainty can get in the way of growth and possibility. Certainty can keep people stuck and unhappy—although trying to make themselves believe they are content.

There are so many people chasing significance. That was me for so many years. I was getting the degrees and certifications; I wanted to be the smartest person in the room to feel important, to feel significant. Some people judge significance by money in the bank, the car they drive, or the zip code they live in. Many people judge it by the number of followers one has on social media. The world appears to be passionate about spotlighting some people and making them untouchable idols. There is a new generation that truly believes they can go live on their phone in an app and create such a following of fans that they can make millions, be famous, and be important. Because that is what they have watched happen to many.

Instead of being an influencer, let's be people of influence through God's light and love shining through us. We need to look different and show up differently than what the world says is important.

What Does the Bible Say about What We Should Focus On?

Instead of striving for more, more, more, what if we traded that mindset for acceptance and gratitude for what we already have and what God is working out for us that we can't even imagine yet! Luke 16:10 says, "Whoever can be trusted with very little can also be trusted with much…" (NIV). That did not say God wants us to have little. It demonstrates that when we are good stewards, then we can have even more opportunities to grow that trust. Let's celebrate and appreciate what God is orchestrating through our gratitude and obedience!

Your Values Are Not in Your Valuables

James 1:5 says, "If any of you lacks wisdom, you should ask God, who gives **generously** to all without finding fault, and it will be given to you" (NIV, emphasis mine). We are seeking wisdom when we seek His Kingdom! Make God the CEO of your life, and he will make you CFO of your finances.

What would a CEO expect of the CFO? Not just maintenance, but multiplication! I love the parable starting in Matthew 25:14 about the bags of gold. We can pull a lot about trust and faith from that parable. The master trusted his servants, empowered them with opportunity, and had faith in their decision-making. Remember, it says, "according to his ability." What are we doing with the blessings and opportunities God gives us? Please don't bury it, please don't be fearful, and please don't waste it!

When the world wants certainty, the Word preaches love. What makes me chuckle is that love is the most uncertain thing around! Is there any guarantee that someone will receive your love? Love you back? Love you unconditionally? Give love in return? The world may question how we can love a God we can't physically see. Yet, our greatest commandment of all is to love the Lord our God with all our heart, with all our soul, and with all our mind. That's quite contrary to the world's need for certainty.

And lastly, instead of chasing significance, the Bible demonstrates how we are called to a contributing and giving heart. This is one of my personal favorite side effects of God's love! I want to be a purposeful contributor to other's lives. To teach, encourage, help, and give in any way I can. I see it as an extension of Jesus's hands and feet, and it's a blessing to have the opportunity to pour into others and a gift to me when I can see a positive impact for someone else.

See, running after significance is quite self-focused and self-serving. Contributing to others is about them, not ourselves. It fulfills my purpose of being of service to others. In what ways can you see more opportunities to contribute and give? God blesses us with time, talents, and treasures and it is not meant for those to be kept to ourselves. He blessed us with these things to share as a blessing to others. You can't outgive God! Give it away! Contribute toward others and just see what happens in your own life! And that is Kingdom-mindedness when focusing on contributing and giving to others.

I am on a quest to be zealous for good works, to be a cheerful giver, and to contribute toward others by finding ways to build them up, connect them with others that can help in their lives or their business, to be part of what makes up strong communities, strong in faith. Will you join me?

God is an abundant God and always has been. Ever since "In the beginning...." Deuteronomy 8:18a says, "It is he who gives you the ability to produce wealth" (NIV). Not greedy for money but eager to serve others with it.

When we contrast what the world deems as important and what the Bible says is the way, it just appears so obvious to me. The world focuses on what it wants; we should aim to focus on, with gratitude, what we already have and what we will be blessed with. Make wise decisions. Seek God's will first. Break free from worldly thinking. Be generous. Seek the Kingdom. Trust God. Have faith in His plans.

Your Kingdom assignment needs your mind and finances to be in order. We can't be utilized greatly and have incredible impact on others if we are busy working seventy hours a week and half of our take-home pay is going toward paying back debt. You may need to pray for God to break stronghold beliefs of previous generations or even help to free you from living in the past or reliving past hurts. Those things often show up in our finances (or lack thereof).

If we are truly living in Him, then there is no place for worry (lack of faith) and there is no place for doubt (lack of trust). Your identity is in Christ the Lord, not in your job, your home, or your things.

Kristi Nowrouzi
Author, Mortgage Advisor
www.buildanagent.com

CHAPTER 29

OUR DAILY WORK—
A HOLY CALLING TO STEWARDSHIP—
SERVING THE LORD FULL TIME

Jan Sturesson

God was the first to work. This is why work is holy and spiritual. Traditional work (non-church work) is not secular; it is spiritual and holy! In six days, the Lord created all of creation, and on that sixth day, He created the crown of His creation: man. Then He said, "Tomorrow we rest." There is a rhythm of *rest* in creation for everything—people, land, money, and assets. To *work in rest* is to receive your gifts and talents from the Lord. It is to understand your privilege to co-create with the Creator and fulfill your calling in your daily work, allowing the Lord to take care of the results. This is freedom and quality of work!

In Matthew 21:1–2, we read of Jesus entering Jerusalem. He "traveled" on a donkey. He told the disciples to get a donkey and a donkey's colt. They were instructed that if anyone asked why they were taking them, they should say that "the Lord has need of them." If we look upon the donkey as the beast of burden and a picture of working life, it is interesting that Jesus said to "give Me the donkey. I have a need for it." The real rest in work and in our working life is to *give it to the Lord*.

Out of this parable, let us ask some thought-provoking questions:

- Do you give your "donkey" (your working life) to the Lord daily or do you just give Him Sunday mornings?
- Do you understand that Jesus is interested in your professional work and your profession?

- Are you ready to let Jesus sit on your donkey, so He can take control, lead, and manage your working life?

Linked to these questions, let's conclude that our work is *a divine calling* to the stewardship of creation. We should serve God "full time" in our daily work—in whatever we are called to do. Teacher, carpenter, consultant, medical doctor, CEO, or plumber—it's all supposed to be done with Him! The Bible contains many role models in different industries and professions. Deborah was a judge; Luke was a medical doctor; Joseph was a steward and political leader; a later Joseph, and Jesus, were both carpenters. Exodus 36 has some interesting workers: "And Bezalel and Aholiab, and every gifted artisan in whom the Lord has put wisdom and understanding, to know how to do all manner of work for the service of the sanctuary, shall do according to all that the Lord has commanded" (Exodus 36:1 NKJV).

So, there is a calling from the Lord to all of us. God has a plan for each one of us. If He called you, He will provide what you need. God does *not* call the equipped, skillful, and gifted. He gives gifts, He equips, and He gives us skills.

Romans 12:1–2 says: "I beseech you therefore, brethren, by the mercies of God, that you *present your bodies a living sacrifice*, holy, acceptable to God, which is your reasonable service. And *do not be conformed to this world*, but be transformed by the renewing of your mind, that you may prove what is that good and acceptable and perfect will of God" (NKJV, emphasis mine). What does this mean? It is about giving everything you have—*skills, talent, money, relationships, ideas, and time*—to the Lord while you take on the role of being a steward in His service. If you seek His face and will, you will understand God's DNA.

If you listen, He will speak. If you obey, He will act!

When you can take responsibility for your calling and ask the Holy Spirit to lead you in your daily work, you will become a blessing to the world.

There is a huge difference between a nurse, police officer, or CEO that just does their job and people in the same positions with a calling from the Lord.

It is easy to conform to today's world. For instance, you can be conformed in your values, wondering: *What is life? What is a human being? How will technology (regarding AI and robots) impact ethical issues? What is true wisdom and knowledge?* But the truth can only be found in God. He alone has the solutions we are looking for.

The Bible also says, "For all the promises of God in Him are Yes, and in Him Amen, to the glory of God through us" (2 Corinthians 1:20 NKJV).

The question is: What is God's *yes* to our area, industry, or profession? If we seek the Lord, we will find inspiration and answers in the Bible, both generally and specifically. We need to interpret, understand, and discern today's trends and weak signals—and then find God's solutions to today's problem: God's *yes!*—professionally and spiritually. This will glorify God through us!

Back to the garden of Eden! The Lord gave man a very clear task on a specific plot of land—the garden of Eden—between four rivers. This was before the fall of man in sin, so all of it was good. The Lord said to Adam and Eve, "This is your garden (your specially designed calling and place) to tend and keep and multiply, so be stewards and take responsibility." God is still saying the same thing today. So, the final question is this: Have we found our garden or are we lost in the wilderness?

(For *Workplace Theology*, turn to Appendix A.)

Jan Sturesson
International Chairman of the International Christian Chamber of Commerce
www.iccc.net

CHAPTER 30

VISIONARY VENTURES: ANTICIPATING THE FUTURE OF KINGDOM COMMERCE

Steve Ahearn

The future of Kingdom commerce, while being a fun topic for discussion, is fundamental to keeping the United States a "nation under God." People are struggling to cope with the accelerated pace of life and the challenges of new technology. Mental health issues, loneliness, and suicide rates are all increasing, while church attendance and faith is rapidly decreasing. The places that house the answers to our societal problems are being ignored. Why is that? Part of the answer is that a large part of the population no longer believes in an absolute and universal truth. They don't want to sit in church on a Sunday morning to hear that God is the Truth and has requirements to be His follower. Another part of the problem is that in our "on demand" world, people can get anything they want delivered to their door at their convenience. So, they are looking for an "on demand" God too. They want God-Prime. Pray a prayer and have the answer delivered in twenty-four hours with the option to return it, if the answer isn't exactly what they had in mind.

Without a universal truth, agreed upon by the vast majority of the population, there is no way for society to function long term. If morality is removed from the decision-making process, then we become a nation of laws—only laws. Laws with no fixed underpinnings. The legal system becomes the new religion and the arbiter of good and evil. The best lawyers are godlike because they can bend the laws to the advantage of their clients. This is temporary. Because the laws are not based on a moral code, they will break down; without the code, the law will disintegrate over time. Then comes chaos.

What does this have to do with the future of Kingdom commerce? Everything. If society needs the healing that only God can provide, but they are not willing to go to a church to receive the answers they need to be whole, where do they get that information? Correct—from the Kingdom merchants. Small businesses employ over 46 percent of the American workforce. That is over 81 million people! There are 400 million small businesses in the world. There are almost 110 million credit card transactions per day in America, and over 1 billion worldwide. So what? Those numbers prove that all businesses are in the people business. People who may not go to church, people who may be struggling, who may be looking for answers.

Imagine how impactful Kingdom businesses can be. Imagine *81 million* people going to work for a Bible-based company five days a week. Imagine consumers seeing merchants who are making a good living and are happy and fair and can be trusted and are also forthright in their faith. That silent witnessing multiplied across millions of transactions could have a dynamic impact on the spiritual health of the country. Kingdom commerce can be the daily example of God's good work to the masses. Successful, content, happy merchants could be the magnet that attracts those who are searching for an answer. This "sneaky evangelism" would have a huge impact on the unsaved. They would be able to see God in action—in lives well-lived—before ever stepping into a church. Seeing what God can do will break down barriers and soften hearts.

What has to happen to bring this to fruition? First, we have to hold Kingdom businesses accountable. A Kingdom merchant has to be above reproach and fair in all dealings. This isn't about throwing a fish on an ad and hoping to attract the Christians. This is about conducting your business in alignment with biblical principles. Second, we need to create a safe harbor, so that businesses can feel empowered to share their faith. A merchant should be able to move forward in their faith without fear of offending someone and being shouted down in the public square that is social media. Third, Christan consumers need to feel compelled to frequent the Kingdom businesses, even if they are a little less convenient. And finally, the merchant needs to share their rewards with Kingdom organizations, so that the good work can be expanded.

Engaging in *values-based commerce* is a win for everyone. The merchant can grow their business by creating relationships that extend beyond the transactional levels. These relationships will increase repeat and referral business and decrease customer acquisition expenses. That is the perfect trifecta for all businesses. The customer wins because they can align their spending with their values at the transactional level. The more consumers that trade with Kingdom businesses, the greater the influence they bring to the market. By uniting behind the economic might that the Christian consumer possesses, great changes can be made across the entire system. As mainstream businesses lose customers and revenue to the Kingdom-based businesses, they will become very open to making corporate changes that align with Christian values.

If Christian consumers would band together and put the full weight of their economic heft to support Kingdom businesses—and if those businesses remain true to biblical principles, together they will influence and change the current economic structure. Millions of workers and customers conducting millions of transactions will be witnesses of Jesus to the world at a basic, everyday, real-life level. The future of Kingdom commerce, in some very tangible ways, is one of the most important factors in determining the success of the United States itself.

Steve Ahearn
Founder, Talents Rewards
www.talentsrewards.com

CALL TO ACTION
WHAT'S NEXT FOR "KINGDOM COMMERCE—LEADERS IMPACTING CULTURE THROUGH FAITH AND ACTION"?

As you come to the end of *Kingdom Commerce*, know that it's not a conclusion but the start of an impactful and inspired journey ahead. The narratives and insights you've encountered from our remarkable authors are more than stories; they are a powerful call to action for you to live out your faith with resilience and intentionality, blending it seamlessly with your business endeavors.

The experiences you read about are fundamentally human. As we encounter people in business—vendors, customers, and even employees—let these stories serve as a reminder that not everyone may be at the same place in their journey. Exhibiting compassion, love, and grace in our interactions can become the spark that ignites a curiosity in others about God. Through our understanding, patience, and willingness to meet people where they are, we can truly reflect the heart of the Kingdom in the marketplace.

Our mission goes beyond the conventional realms of profit and loss. We are called to impact culture through faith and action for Kingdom advancement. Equipped with the wisdom from these pages, you are poised to transform not only your workplace but the entire marketplace.

Accept this invitation to delve deeper and connect with the authors, who are all accessible through our website. Your active participation in this nationwide movement is invaluable. As we know, there's strength in numbers, and when united, our impact multiplies.

Join us at the U.S. Christian Chamber of Commerce and be part of a collective force driving positive change throughout the nation. Together, our endeavors in advancing the Kingdom through the marketplace, strengthening Christian businesses, and transforming cities will have a lasting impact.

Thank you for joining us on this journey of transformation, wisdom, and victory in Christ. May God bless you abundantly as you live out your faith in the pursuit of His Kingdom.

Krystal Parker

President, U.S. Christian Chamber of Commerce

APPENDIX A
WORKPLACE THEOLOGY: A PROCLAMATION FOR REFORMATION THROUGH A SPIRITUAL WORKERS MOVEMENT

Jan Sturesson

Work – in the beginning.

- God was the first person who worked.

  He worked by creating the universe, the earth, and man. God created mankind—*male and female*—in His own image and to the crown of creation! (Genesis 1:1, 2:2, 1:26).

- God planted a Garden and "put" man in it.

  It was a chosen area for man to dwell in, in order to express his creativity (Genesis 2:8).

- Work was intended as a delight before God.

  In a paradise environment—where creativity brings purpose, peace, and joy.

- In the beginning, work was good and honorable in itself—*in doing something for someone.* It was a fulfilling activity, together with God, not a toil performed in man's own strength (Proverbs 8:29–31).

Work – became slavery.

- Through the fall, by eating the forbidden fruit, man chose independence from God and a consequence was that work turned into slavery!

  "In the sweat of your face you shall eat your bread" (Genesis 3:19).

- The whole creation groans and labours, waiting for the revelation of the children of God (Romans 8:22). Creation longs to be delivered from its slavery under corruption and to experience the freedom of the children of God, i.e., a restoration to how things were at the beginning (Romans 8:18).

Work – redeemed in Christ.
- Through the death and resurrection of Jesus Christ, God has provided a way back to unbroken fellowship with God—including our everyday work. Through believing with our heart in Jesus Christ, we are justified, and through the confession of our mouth we are saved—born again—from a meaningless life and burdensome work. God has delivered us from the power of darkness and conveyed us into the Kingdom of the Son of His love—the Kingdom of God (Romans 10:9; Colossians 1:13).
- God has through Christ redeemed ALL—even our work. There are legal grounds for a reconciled and restored work together with the Father, through Jesus Christ, and in the power of the Holy Spirit (Colossians 1:20; 2 Corinthians 5:17–18).

Work – to steward and develop in co-creation with God.
- Man was created to co-create.
  Man's mission was to co-create with God, based upon an unbroken relationship with Him. Work was practical and organized, e.g., Adam gave names to all the animals (Genesis 2:20), or today when scientists discovered photons.
- God gave man two practical commissions:
  - To cultivate, tend, and keep, and to enjoy the creation (Genesis 2:15).
  - To multiply and fill the earth (Genesis 1:27–28).

- In the Garden, work is performed to the glory of God. Through this we move away from our self-centeredness, and we create (serve/produce) things, which other people need (Colossians 3:17).

Work – with a purpose and according to a plan.
- God wants to use our work and working life for His purposes. Jesus rode into Jerusalem on a donkey, a beast of burden. The donkey is an image for our working life in slavery being released to serve the Lord, where He may ride on our donkeys manifesting God's Kingdom in our time (Matthew 21:1–2).
- The Lord has a plan for us—in line with His calling upon us (Romans 8:28; Psalm 139:16). He has equipped us for our purpose and mission (Romans 12:6–8).
- The Lord will use His people to stand in the gap (taking responsibility) for those things He has already given His YES to (representing His will). This is also true about big issues in the spheres of working life and society. This way the blessings given to His people will become a blessing to other people, their workplaces, cities, and nations.

Work – a holy calling and a full-time ministry for God.
- There is a call and a commission—a unique plan—for every believer (Psalm 139:14–16; Romans 8:28–30).
- All work and all assignments in the Kingdom are a full-time service for God.
  This is true regardless of the type of work we do. (The royal priesthood of 1 Peter 2:9.)
- In the Kingdom of God, there is no such thing as secular work. Work is in itself spiritual, and a perfectly satisfactory service performed in fellowship with God (Colossians 3:17).

Work – a service before God.
- Work is a service before God (Genesis 1:26–28; Romans 12:1–2).
- Work is a worship of the Creator. It is a grateful response from the heart to God for the personality, gifts, and talents that He has given us to express our creative purpose.
- We are called to look upon our work with enjoyment and pleasure before God.

  This is about us being granted the privilege to live in an unbroken relationship with the Lord.

Work – a fragrance of God's Kingdom.
- The Kingdom of God is expressed through believers seeking the rule of God.

  The people of God (*ecclesia*) are offered the opportunity to receive by faith the restoration of a working life in the power of the Holy Spirit (Ephesians 1:7–12).
- We are called to manifest the hope of a complete restoration.

  This is to be a foretaste of the coming glory (Ephesians 1:12). We are called to live in the world, but not be of it, and to be salt and light in it! (Matthew 5:16).
- Through faith in Jesus Christ, God has made a garden accessible for every human being to tend and keep. This is a place where our talents and gifts are put to use, and where we can make a useful contribution, without wearing out either ourselves or the creation (Colossians 1:19–20).
- There is a dimension of glory that comprises all work in the Kingdom of God.

  This is a "fragrance" of the coming King and a testimony about Him, without words (2 Corinthians 2:14).

Work – a walk of faith.
- There is a life of freedom in the Holy Spirit.
  The Bible says: "Not by might, nor by power, but by My Spirit, says the Lord of hosts" (Zechariah 4:6). The flesh—own ambitions, efforts, and reasoning without Him—have no place (John 6:63).
- It is about a walk in faith together with the Lord, and about building on the rock. This means hearing the word from the Lord and obeying it (Matthew 7:24–26).
- Everything birthed by God has the ability to multiply.
  Expect development of your work like the mustard seed. This is because it carries life (1 John 5:4).

Work – based on His YES.
- There is a God's "Yes and Amen" to all of our work and life.
  - Through Jesus Christ, God has given us His YES and AMEN to our work (2 Corinthians 1:20).
- God has a solution (YES) to every human problem located in Jesus Christ.
  The problem is that this solution is "hidden" in Christ and is only accessible through faith in Him and by the guidance of the Holy Spirit (2 Corinthians 1:20).

Work – in rest through faith.
- To work in rest is now possible together with the Lord.
  According to Hebrews, it is possible to enter into God's rest and to work from that position (Hebrews 4:3, 9–10). We may cast our burdens on the Lord who has promised to care for us. His yoke is easy, and His burden is light! (Psalm 55:22; Matthew 6:25–34, 11:30).
- Unless the Lord builds the house, the workers labour in vain; unless the Lord guards the city, the watchman stays awake in

vain ... for so He gives His beloved sleep (walking in rest and not in your own power through pushing and stress) (Psalm 127:1–2).
- When we do what we are destined for—i.e., do what we are, instead of being what we do—our journey with the Lord will be made easier. We rest in relation to the results of our work. Therefore, we are not lazy nor inactive, but it is the Lord who gives the fruit in terms of the result.

Work – when God is our Provider and our Employer.
- If we seek the Kingdom of God first, all the other things we need shall be added to us. Work in the Kingdom of God is not directly connected to a salary or wage. We work through faith in God and trust that His promises are true (Matthew 6:25–34).
- Scripture also tells us that the laborer is worthy of his hire (Luke 10:7; 1 Timothy 5:18), and also that those who do not work shall not eat. This should, however, only be understood from the perspective that work is "doing something for someone" and not about a typical labor for a salary.

Work – brings maturity and sanctification through His mercy and care.
- God has a claim on all creation and wants to restore it. This includes you as well as your working life. He brings us to the ends of ourselves through various tests and trials, so that those things we are and do will come from the Spirit. He renews us so that the fruit of the Spirit becomes visible in our lives. Where the Spirit of the Lord is, there is liberty! (2 Corinthians 3:17; Galatians 2:20).
- The trial process is God's quality assurance of our life and work. We are brought through death to life! God follows the

same pattern as with Abraham, who was circumcised in his flesh as a sign of the covenant. His calling was to become a father of many people. But it was only after the circumcision that he was able to bear forth the seed that produced a son according to the promise—Isaac (Genesis 17:1–14). Like Abraham, we will all be circumcised in the area of our calling; however, in the New Covenant, this is a circumcision of the heart (Galatians 5:6).

- When Jesus has full control of us, there is no limit to what He can do through us!

"With God, all things are possible." (MATTHEW 19:26)
"Of the increase of His government and peace, there shall be no end!" (ISAIAH 9:7)

APPENDIX B
CONTRIBUTING AUTHORS IN ALPHABETICAL ORDER

Steve Ahearn
Founder, Talents Rewards
www.talentsrewards.com

Steve has spent the majority of his four-decade career in the banking and mortgage industry. He has held multiple positions, including regional, divisional, and national roles with Fortune 200 companies. He has also owned and operated—and sold—several small businesses. All of this experience has led to the formation of Talents Rewards, a universal rewards program that introduces Christian businesses to consumers who want to live their values system at the transactional level. Steve and his wife, Valerie, reside in Charlotte, North Carolina, and have two adult children.

Shelsea Becker
Founder and President of LYN Ministries
www.lynministries.org

As the founder and president of LYN Ministries, Shelsea merges her roles as a speaker, author, and comedic host to inspire and uplift audiences. Founding the She Will Conference and Girl's Weekend God's Way, she empowers women in their faith journey, while her directorial debut in Christian country music videos adds a creative dimension to her life as a wife and mother, balancing family, faith, and a passion for entertainment. You can contact her at www.lynministries.org.

Simon Bois a.k.a. "Florida Night Train"

Author, Senior Executive Corporate Director
www.facebook.com/FloridaNightTrain

Simon has been published since year 2000 in both Canada and the U.S., and in French and English. Simon's humble beginning as a photographer for Toronto-based *L'Express* magazine grew into photojournalism. Eventually, Simon became "Florida Night Train," featuring columns about the lifestyles of celebrities and high-profile individuals, like the legendary Ted Nugent, Bill Davidson Jr. (Harley Davidson), Danica Patrick, Jesse James (West Coast Choppers), Paul Teutul Sr. (Orange County Choppers), Billy Lane (Choppers, Inc.), Paul Cox (Indian Larry), Mondo (Denver's Choppers), Jason Chinnock (CEO Ducati), Joanna Olsen (CEO Coyote Ugly), and so many more.

Seeking to write about life's values from his interviewees' perspectives, Simon inspires his readers and has published in *Florida Women*, *HOG*, *Born to Ride* and *Full Throttle Magazine*, and *Florida, Ride or Die* magazines, and at www.NSAEN.com. The proud father of three children, Trinity, Jade, and Eric, Simon also enjoys life as a successful independent senior executive corporate director and VP sales for small- to medium-sized corporations.

Simon can be personally reached at seboisfnt@gmail.com.

Jim and Martha Brangenberg

Co-Founders iWork4Him
www.iWork4Him.com

Jim and Martha Brangenberg committed their lives to full-time ministry as teenagers and later recognized that their workplace answered that call. As entrepreneurs and business owners, Jim and Martha learned their work was significant in the

Kingdom of God and able to reach people who would never set foot in a church. Since 2013, Jim and Martha have co-hosted the iWork4Him talk show challenging thousands across the globe with the simple message that your workplace *is* your mission field. They have added podcasts for iRetire4Him and sheWorks4Him into their line-up. In addition to the podcasts and radio spots, speaking, and mentoring, they have co-authored the collaborative books of *iWork4Him*, *sheWorks4Him*, and *iRetire4Him*, and are leading a project to facilitate collaboration across the country. Learn more about Jim, Martha, and iWork4Him at www.iWork4Him.com.

Joy Capps
Author, Podcaster
www.joycapps.com

Joy Capps helps Christian business leaders use marketing communications in alignment with *The Ultimate How-to Guide* (a.k.a. the Bible) without hype or manipulation. Her God-given message permeates her collaborations, podcasts (*The Joyful Communications Podcast* and *The Kingdom Driven Entrepreneur Live Podcast*, in which she is a co-host). She also wrote *Joyful Copy—How to Show Up in the Marketplace Ethically and Authentically*. Those who encounter her say Joy embodies her name with her enthusiasm, drive, determination, and love for the Lord.

Nate Chrisman
Founder and CEO of I Want Good
www.iwantgood.org

Nate, his wife, Mindy, and their five children reside in Ohio. Nate is the founder and CEO of I Want Good, a brand that focuses on lifestyle, curriculum strategy, and resources aimed at empowering youth in public schools throughout the U.S. The brand equips young people with the necessary tools and mindset to make good decisions and build a life they love. Nate and his team are driven to equip students to become resilient and "Ready for Life." Their unique community-based school strategy, fueled by their non-profit organization, THE**CLEFT**, delivers critical support to teens, schools, and communities, and is impacting thousands of students and communities nationwide. *The Cleft, Non-Profit for Youth—GOOD-LIFE, School Strategy & Curriculum Resources.*

Nicole L. Davis, PhD

Co-Founder of Empower to Engage
www.empowertoengage.com
www.evewhereareyou.com

Nicole has a passion for family, women, and leadership development. She is a wife of over three decades, and mother of two adult sons. Dr. Davis is a U.S. Navy veteran, a certified mediator, and a harassment prevention expert. She is also co-founder of Empower to Engage, a mediation, coaching, and consulting firm located in Owings Mills, Maryland.

Joy Dawson

Founder of Joyfully Planned Firm
www.joyfullyplanned.com

Joy Dawson is a distinguished entrepreneur, strategic visionary, and founder of Joyfully Planned Firm—a dynamic entity that has seamlessly transformed from an event company into a formidable business development force. With a passion for connecting people and a keen insight into the intricacies of commerce, Joy has become a driving force in the world of Kingdom commerce.

As a Kingdom connection strategist, Joy brings a unique blend of talents, educational background, and business acumen to the forefront. Her commitment to fostering connections that transcend the ordinary has earned her recognition as a thought leader in the realm of commerce.

A dynamic force in the business world, Joy Dawson continues to shape the landscape of Kingdom commerce with her innovative approaches, dedication to excellence, and an unwavering commitment to fostering meaningful connections. Her biography serves as a testament to the remarkable journey of a visionary leader in the pursuit of commerce aligned with purpose. She prays you, too, FIND JOY!

Dana Dunmyer

President and CEO of TQI Solutions
www.tqi.solutions.com
Dana.A.Dunmyer@TQI.Solutions

In 1995, Dana left behind a thriving pastoral ministry in California, and founded CAD-COM Consulting, a technology development firm. What started as a one-man operation quickly flourished into a powerhouse with over three hundred dedicated professionals. In a remarkable turn of events, CADCOM was eventually acquired by a prestigious Venture Capital firm in Omaha. After this success, Dana, his wife, Connie, and their exceptional executive team heeded the call, and founded what is now known as TQI Solutions, a trusted partner for over three hundred clients spanning across various sectors. From Fortune 500 companies to smaller enterprises, TQI's global client base stretches across the world. Notable clients such as GE, International Paper, Snecma Aerospace, Deloitte & Touché, Citi, Duke University Medical Center, and Lockheed Martin rely on TQI for innovative technology solutions and services in their own diverse industries.

Dana and Connie also founded the Beracha Foundation, a non-profit organization. The foundation plays a pivotal role in granting funds and providing financial services to non-profits, ministries, start-ups, and visionary businesses. Through their unique approach, they generously offer up to $4.35 for every $1.00 contributed by these entities towards enterprise software, marketing, design, and consulting solutions offered by TQI. Since its inception in 2000, TQI's Beracha Fund grants have generated an astonishing $48 million, making cutting-edge technology affordable for businesses and organizations in need, while shaping a brighter future.

Eric Floyd
Entertainer, Author, Podcast Producer
Eric.floyd@uschristianchamber.com

Eric is an entertainer at Universal Orlando, an ambassador for both the Central Florida Christian Chamber of Commerce and the U.S. Christian Chamber of Commerce, a contributing turf writer for *Gaming and Destinations* magazine (in Louisville, Kentucky), and the producer and host of the Christian podcast *Where Grace Abounds*, which can be heard wherever you listen to your favorite podcasts! Check out the *Where Grace Abounds* podcast.

Robert Fukui
Marketing Executive, Author, Co-Founder Power Couples by Design
www.marriedentrepreneur.com
RFukui@i61BusinessDevelopment.com
Podcast: *Thriving in Tandem* https://marriedentrepreneur.co/blog

Robert received his marketing degree from San Jose State University and experienced twenty-five successful years in sales and marketing with companies such as Coca-Cola, Novartis

Pharmaceutical, and Bristol-Myers Squibb. He played instrumental roles in the launch of six major brands, directly responsible for over $250 million in revenue, and has been the recipient of national sales and leadership awards. His business acumen allows him to help family businesses build a more profitable, efficient, and sustainable company. Together with his wife, Kay, they have developed an innovative consulting program, Power Couples by Design™, which equips the married entrepreneur to build a thriving marriage *and* a prosperous business. They have also authored the book, *Tandem: The Married Entrepreneurs' Guide for Greater Work-Life Balance*.

Robert and Kay Lee have a heart to see Kingdom business families thrive in every facet of their lives, but also want to be a catalyst for building strong Kingdom business communities. They see seminars, workshops, and mastermind groups as the recipe for building strong entrepreneurial communities that transform lives and are dedicated to Kingdom growth.

Chet Gladkowski

Created National Day of Hope
www.nationaldayofhope.net

Chet came out of the insurance technology industry and created the National Day of Hope to share and train people in spreading hope through Jesus. His latest hopeful resource, *PhD in Hope*, is available on Amazon. Email: info@nationaldayofhope.net/

Virginia Grounds
Author, Founder/Publisher of Breakthrough Christian Publishing
www.breakthroughchristianpublishing.com
www.virginiagrounds.net

Virginia is an author, speaker, podcaster, Bible teacher, publisher, and former radio host. She serves in the local church in women's ministry leadership, is a project manager for HigherLife Publishing & Marketing, and founder of Breakthrough Christian Publishing. The mission of Breakthrough Christian Publishing is to publish books with a Kingdom mindset. Virginia is an Advanced Writers & Speakers Association (AWSA) certified coach and speaker, as well as a certified professional publisher from the Nonfiction Authors Association (NFAA). She served for twenty years alongside her husband in full-time ministry as co-founder and operations director, helping law enforcement and first responders meet the needs of hurting people through chaplaincy. Before serving the Christian community, she was in leadership in the corporate world as a production director and event coordinator.

Morris Hartley
President, H & H Products Company
www.hhproductscompany.com
morris@hhproductscompany.com

Morris Hartley, a dynamic leader and entrepreneur, currently serves as the President of H & H Products Company based in Orlando, Florida. Stepping into the role within the family business founded by his father, Len Hartley, in 1964, Morris brings a wealth of experience and dedication to the company's continued success. Beyond his professional endeavors, Morris actively serves on the board of the Fellowship of Christian Athletes, the International Beverage Dispensing

Equipment Association (IBDEA), and his local church. He is married to Lisa and has two sons, two daughters, a daughter-in-law, and very soon, a grandson, all of whom he cherishes dearly.

Craig Hohnberger

Keynote Speaker, Business Coach
www.bujiactioncoach.com

Craig Hohnberger gave his life to Jesus after a marketplace encounter. He is a dad, husband, and an entrepreneur in the franchising and business coaching (and training) industries. As a keynote speaker, he has addressed audiences in nine different countries.

Kristi Nowrouzi

Author, Mortgage Advisor
www.buildanagent.com
info@BuildAnAgent.com

Kristi Nowrouzi is a dedicated advocate for financial literacy and is committed to helping people understand their relationship with money. Kristi boasts a wealth of expertise with more than twenty-three years in real estate and finance, thirteen of those years as a mortgage loan officer, and has recently launched a training platform for new real estate agents.

Kristi has published two books and also hosts a popular podcast called *Credit Coaching by Kristi*. Beyond her professional accomplishments, Kristi actively contributes to her community by volunteering at non-profit organizations that are helping our community's must vulnerable and serves as a member of the board of directors for IDignity.

She holds several leadership positions in various networking organizations and loves connecting with great people.

Krystal Parker
President, U.S. Christian Chamber of Commerce
www.uschristianchamber.com

Krystal Parker is a former executive for a Fortune 200 publicly traded oil and gas company. She has over twenty-five years' experience in organizational management leading hundreds of employees, and provided J.D. Powers award-winning customer service to more than 2.1 million customers across the U.S. A former college dropout, Parker advanced her education at Harvard Business School for senior executive leaders, focusing on innovation, globalization, and leadership diversity.

She earned an undergraduate degree in psychology and a master's in marketing. As a certified DISC Personality Test™ behavioral specialist, trainer, speaker, and coach, Parker opened a boutique consulting company, Intent & Impact, to help companies increase profit, reduce turnover, and enhance employee engagement. A best-selling author and professor, Krystal teaches graduate- and undergraduate-level courses. She is the president of the U.S. Christian Chamber of Commerce and a board member of both Missionary Ventures International and the Central Florida Christian Chamber.

Krystal considers herself a marketplace missionary with a strategic focus on citywide transformation. She is committed to seeing faith in action in the marketplace and believes that to reach the world, you must reach the city. Krystal is a wife and mother, and devoted follower of Jesus Christ.

Howard Partridge
International Business Coach
President, Phenomenal Products, Inc.
www.howardpartridge.com

Howard Partridge is an international business coach, the founder of Phenomenal Business Coaching Powered by Zig Ziglar, and author of twelve books, including *The Monday Morning Christian—How Living Out Your Faith in Business Leads to Phenomenal Success*. He is the president of Phenomenal Products, Inc., and a best-selling author, conference speaker/trainer.

David Roznowski (Pastor Roz)
Pastor, Founder of West Ohio Christian Chamber of Commerce
wochristianchamber.com
pastorroz@wcoil.com

After twenty-four years in the Ohio Army National Guard, Sergeant First Class Roznowski traded "Sgt. Roz" for "Pastor Roz." He and his wife, Heather, founded the Neighborhood Relief Thrift Store in March 2000, with $500 and the stuff in their basement. A year later at age thirty-seven, God called Roz (and Heather) to salvation through Jesus Christ. The business quickly changed into a ministry that helps thousands each year with free material help as well as the hope of the gospel. In 2017, they created Neighborhood Relief Ministries, a street ministry that travels and distributes free clothes and food, in addition to the gospel, prayer, and worship. (They even have a mobile baptism trailer!)

In 2023, Pastor Roz founded the West Ohio Christian Chamber of Commerce, a growing group of business owners and organizations from seven counties, uniting to bring change to their communities.

Pastor Roz was born (and lives) in Lima, Ohio, and is the father of two daughters. A husband of thirty-two years, father, pastor, chaplain, teaching evangelist, entrepreneur, and executive, Roz likes to simply refer to himself as a servant, soldier, and slave of Jesus Christ.

Dawn Sipley
International Speaker
www.sipleythebest.com

Dawn Sipley is an international speaker, taking the stage hundreds of times over her career. With her twenty years in HR, helping hundreds of companies hire thousands of employees, and negotiating millions of dollars of salaries, Dawn is well-versed in what it takes to create the best team.

William (Bill) Snell Jr.
President, Missionary Ventures International
www.mvi.org

Bill has served thirty-five years in pastoral ministry in California, Oklahoma, Texas, Colorado, and Florida, as well as ten years in banking, real estate, and service industries. Beginning in 2016 and to the present day, Bill serves as president of Missionary Ventures International, headquartered in Maitland, Florida, specializing in serving, equipping, and empowering national Christian leaders in 107 countries. Soon to celebrate his forty-fifth wedding anniversary with Tammy, they enjoy their four adult children and spouses, three grandsons, and four grand-pooches.

Dr. Joshua Steinke

Chiropractor | Steinke Family Chiropractic
Executive Director | Worship Anyway
www.worshipanyway.com
www.Ohiofamilychiropractic.com

Joshua is the father of seven wild children, the husband of the beautiful Mrs. Randee, and a child of the Most High God. He is a chiropractor by trade and has been the owner of Steinke Family Chiropractic in Wapakoneta, Ohio, for twelve years. He is also the director of a street outreach worship ministry called Worship Anyway. Dr. Joshua loves the outdoors and being in God's creation. His testimony is that of Jesus transforming his life from dope dealer to hope dealer. It is his mission to lay hands on the sick and watch them recover, to outwardly worship in every season, and to restore hope in communities through Jesus Christ.

Jan Sturesson

International Chairman of the International Christian Chamber of Commerce
www.iccc.net

Jan Sturesson is International Chairman of the International Christian Chamber of Commerce (ICCC) with members in over seventy nations. The passion of ICCC is to encourage serving the Lord full time in every type of work, and to see an outward manifestation of the inward walk of faith through God's manifest strategies and plans establishing the Kingdom of God in the workplace.

Jan is also the founder of the RESTING—Advice from the Future, an international C-suite consultancy with governments, cities, private sector, and global organizations as clients. His focus is future strategic navigation linked to innovation and leadership. Jan works with projects for the private sector, cities, UN, and the EU Commission. From

2008 to 2015, Jan was the partner and global leader for Government and Public Services Industry, including global organizations, at PwC. The author of over twenty books, he was named one of the fifty most influential people in the world in 2014 on Smart Cities linked to Microsoft's assessment. He has also been serving as an expert to the World Economic Forum (WEF) for many years in the areas of government and urbanization.

Jim Subers
CEO, Vision Orlando
www.visionorlando.org

Jim Subers was born and raised in Miami, and has been married to his beautiful wife, Janice, for over forty years. They met at the University of Florida, where Jim played football for the Gators and got a degree in business management. They have four adult children: one daughter, and three sons, one of them with autism. They have six young grandsons who are among their greatest joys.

Jim and his family have lived around the country and overseas, including Japan for five years. Through his business and ministry, he's been in over forty nations, working in missions, international real estate, oil and gas, church planting, urban youth ministry, audio Bible distribution, prison ministry, teen residential care, and now city transformation. In 2022, he became CEO of Vision Orlando. Their mission is to unite a significant remnant of the *ekklesia* in their community around Jesus, by gathering and mobilizing believing leaders in every arena of influence, including business, government, education, media, arts and entertainment, family, and church. He believes that there is no greater force for good on the earth than this united *ekklesia*.

Ford Taylor
Author, Keynote Speaker, Founder of FSH Strategy Consultants and Transformational Leadership
www.transformlead.com

Ford Taylor is a leadership solutions trainer, strategist, and speaker. With a primary emphasis on the people that serve an organization while simultaneously maintaining a clear focus of the business or organization itself, Ford shares straight-forward practical solutions through authentic leadership training and individualized leadership consulting. With an empathetic intelligence derived from decades of experience with an array of people, personalities, and companies both large and small, Ford helps to both define and navigate leadership in the business culture of today. His trainings and talks are centered on removing constraints, equipping leaders, and empowering people to become happy, successful, high-performing individuals with healthy relationships both inside and outside of the workplace.

As a keynote speaker, Ford Taylor identifies and shares the tools and tactics to develop transformational leaders within every organization at every level. Ford is the founder of FSH Strategy Consultants and Transformational Leadership, author of *Relational Leadership*, and directs a charitable international effort to provide Transformational Leadership to emerging countries worldwide.

Eileen Vazquez
Founder, MS Consulting
www.msconsultingfirm.com
Info@msconsultingfirm.com

MS Consulting Firm is a dynamic start-up business, based in Orlando, Florida, and founded by Eileen Vazquez, a highly experienced HR professional with over two decades of industry expertise. As a minority-owned enterprise, Eileen brings a unique perspective and commitment to providing exceptional human resource solutions.

Her firm aims to cater to the specific needs of small business owners, offering comprehensive services in day-to-day HR tasks, including disciplinary actions, termination guidance, payroll management, and policy development. With a client-centric approach and a deep understanding of the challenges faced by entrepreneurs, MS Consulting Firm is poised to become a trusted partner for businesses seeking reliable, efficient, and compliant HR solutions.

David Welday

Author, President, HigherLife Publishing and Marketing
www.higherlifepublishing.com
dwelday@ahigherlife.com

David is an out-of-the-box thinker, gifted communicator, high-energy motivator, publisher, trainer, marketing strategist, and coach. He is known for his passionate, high-energy demeanor and presentation. He serves as president of HigherLife Publishing and Marketing, a hybrid publishing company, committed to helping clients experience the thrill of making a difference through the messages they share. David is himself a published author and has worked with *New York Times* best-selling authors as well as first-time authors. David has been married to his lovely wife, Amy, more than forty years. Together, they have three grown sons and seven grandchildren.

Bob Willbanks
CEO, G7 Networking
www.g7networking.com or www.ndp-tc.com

Bob Willbanks devotes most of his time to developing the vision of collaborative Kingdom purpose and unity among Christian business professionals. It is his hope and prayer that all G7 Networking participants find encouragement and accountability, enabling them to reach the next rung on their spiritual growth ladder. Through mentoring others and being accountable themselves, Christians in the marketplace can shine God's light into the darkness, living out their lives for Kingdom purpose, rooted and grounded in the absolute truth found only in His Word. Bob's passion is to connect and encourage Christians in business through trust and integrity. G7 plants chapters area by area to create spaces in which Christian professionals can grow together.

A native of Minnesota, Bob began his career with payroll processing before working in sales and marketing. With an inherent knack for creating win-win-win collaborative relationships along with an entrepreneurial spirit, Bob has been blessed by working in HR, real estate, and IT/technical management and consulting. He's owned multiple successful business ventures and has experience with Fortune 500 companies at senior management levels. He and his wife, Barb, also own Next Door Photos in the Twin Cities area.

Most of his adult life, Bob was what he calls, "miserably saved." Even though he considered himself a Christian, he'd never jumped into his faith. That has all changed, and today his focus is on God and his family. Bob wants to use his God-given gifts, talents, and life experiences to pour into others so they can see what is possible—in and through—God. G7 provides a conduit for doing that. His work in G7 enables him to encourage others to jump into the river of their faith too—instead of just dipping their toe in the flowing water. Bob enjoys his quiet time with God and treasures his time with his family and like-minded believers.

IF YOU ENJOYED THIS BOOK, WILL YOU HELP SPREAD THE WORD?

There are several ways you can let others know about this book...

- **Post a 5-Star review on Amazon.**
- **Write about the book in your social media** (Facebook, X, Instagram, LinkedIn – any social media you regularly use!
- **If you podcast or blog**, consider referencing the book, or inviting one of the authors as a guest on your show.
- Recommend the book to friends – word-of-mouth is still the most effective form of advertising.
- **Purchase additional copies** to distribute or sell to your clients, prospects, team members, donors, brokers, dealers, associates, coworkers, family, and friends. Contact HigherLife Publishing and Marketing for bulk orders with a discount at admin@ahigherlife.com.

ABOUT THE U.S. CHRISTIAN CHAMBER OF COMMERCE

Our mission is to build Kingdom, business, and community. We are more than just average people interacting in a beneficial way; we are Christ-following believers building relational capital that can be used to advance the Kingdom, improve lives, grow businesses, and enrich communities. One Nation Under God!

For more information, go to www.uschristianchamber.com or scan this QR Code with your phone.

www.ingramcontent.com/pod-product-compliance
Lightning Source LLC
Chambersburg PA
CBHW062216080426
42734CB00010B/1914